Reading

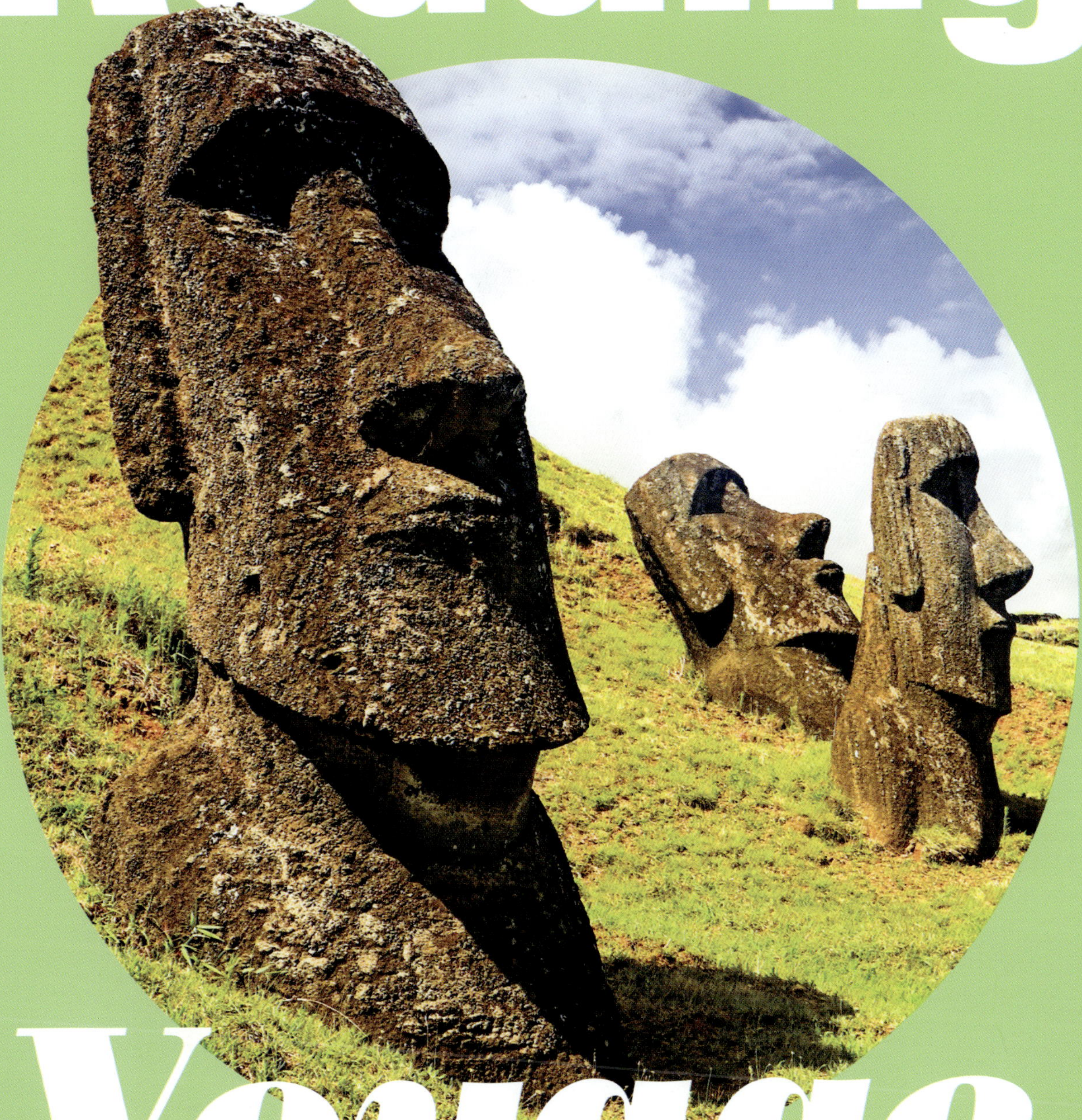

BASIC

Voyage
2

Reading *Voyage*
BASIC 2

Publisher Chung Kyudo
Editors Jeong Yeonsoon, Kim Mina
Authors Milton Prep, Jonathan S. McClelland, Brian Stuart
Proofreader Jonathan S. McClelland
Designer Design Sum

First published in May 2016
By Darakwon, Inc.
Darakwon Bldg., 211, Munbal-ro, Paju-si, Gyeonggi-do 10881
Republic of Korea
Tel: 82-2-736-2031 (Ext. 250)
Fax: 82-2-732-2037

Copyright © 2016 Darakwon, Inc.

All rights reserved. No part of this publication may be reproduced, stored in a retrieval system, or transmitted in any form or by any means, electronic, mechanical, photocopying or otherwise, without the prior consent of the copyright owner. Refund after purchase is possible only according to the company regulations. Contact the above telephone number for any inquiries. Consumer damages caused by loss, damage, etc. can be compensated according to the consumer dispute resolution standards announced by the Korea Fair Trade Commission. An incorrectly collated book will be exchanged.

ISBN 978-89-277-5199-1 58740
        978-89-277-0773-8 58740 (set)

www.darakwon.co.kr

Components Main Book / Workbook
14 13 12 11 10 9 8   24 25 26 27 28

Reading
Voyage

BASIC

2

Unit Components

Before You Read

This section helps students make predictions about the topic by drawing on their background knowledge before reading the passage.

Students can preview the key vocabulary words by checking the ones that they already know.

Main Reading Passage

A focus sentence before each passage gives students tips to help them understand the main idea of the text.

The passages are written to be as interesting and informative as possible, covering a variety of topics. In addition to standard articles, passage formats include short essays, letters, and interviews. This variety of styles helps students become accustomed to reading various types of English texts.

Vocabulary in Context

This section helps students learn the key words from the passage by matching the words with their definitions.

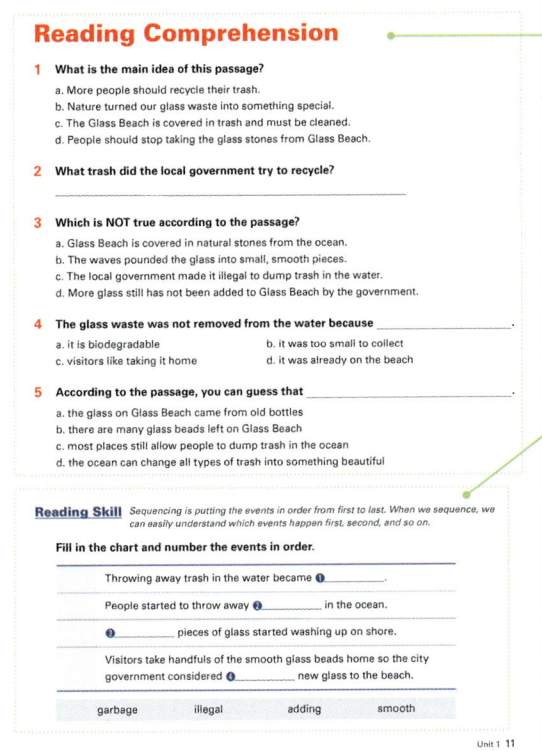

Reading Comprehension

This portion asks students to identify the main idea, details, and draw inferences from the passages through multiple-choice and short-answer questions.

Reading Skill

Students can organize the key concepts of the passage by practicing various reading skills including identifying the main idea, sequencing, cause and effect, and more.

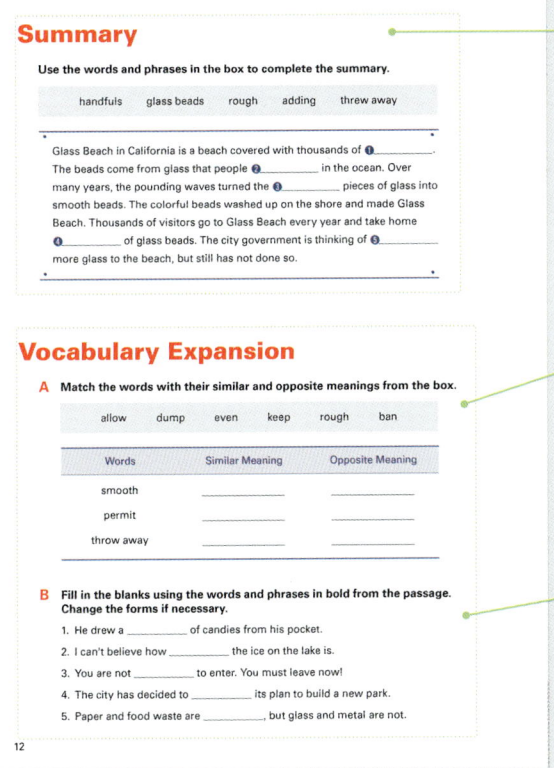

Summary

Students can review the essential information from the passage through the summary.

Vocabulary Expansion

This section presents synonyms, antonyms, prefixes, and suffixes for the key vocabulary words, helping students to expand their vocabularies.

Students can review the key words from the passage in different contexts by completing the sentences.

Workbook — Extra vocabulary and writing practice are provided to enable students to understand the material more deeply.

Online Supplement — MP3 files, answer keys, translations, and vocabulary lists are provided free online at www.darakwon.co.kr. A program for generating vocabulary and writing test sheets is available free online at voca.darakwon.co.kr.

Table of Contents

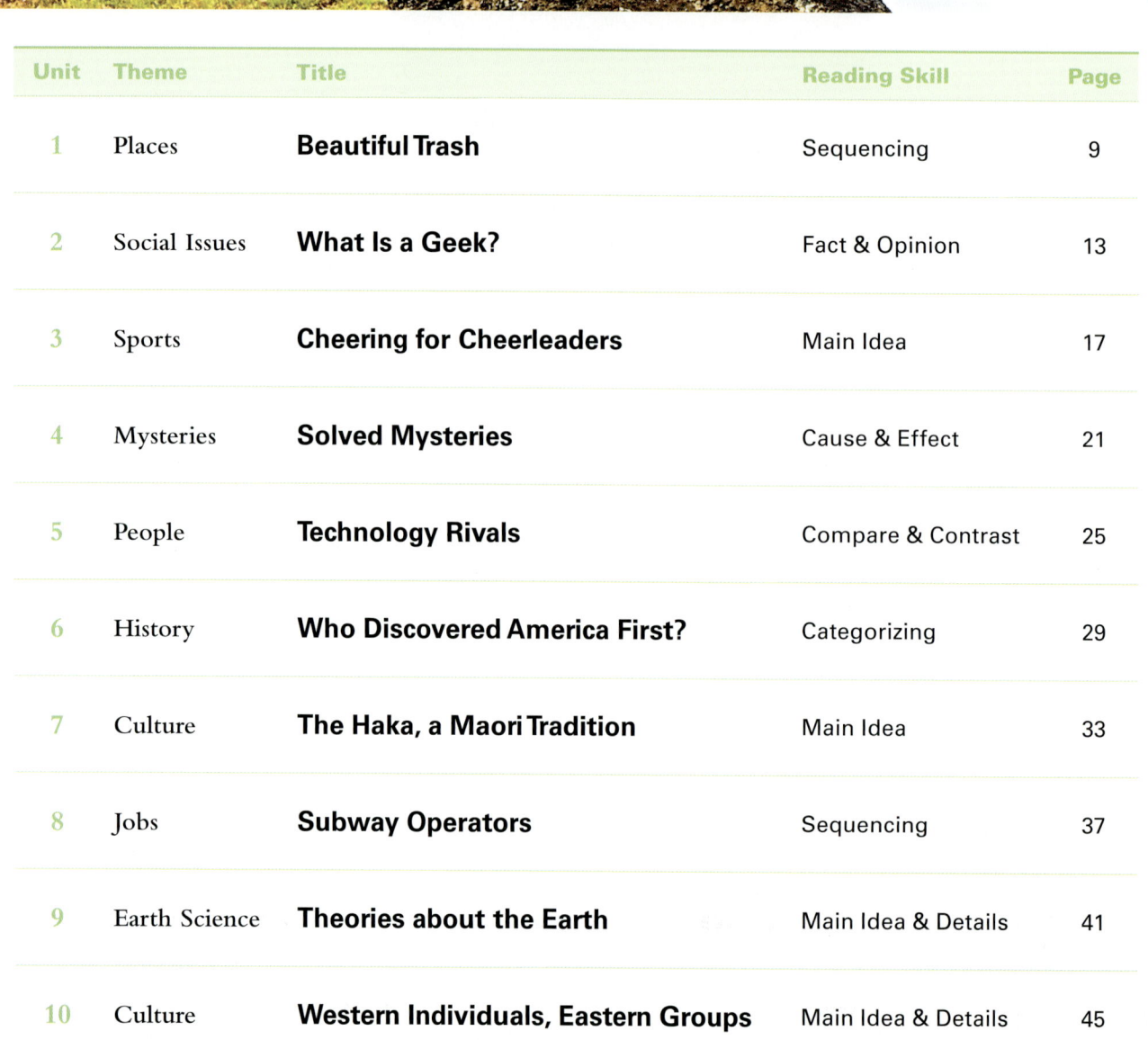

Unit	Theme	Title	Reading Skill	Page
1	Places	**Beautiful Trash**	Sequencing	9
2	Social Issues	**What Is a Geek?**	Fact & Opinion	13
3	Sports	**Cheering for Cheerleaders**	Main Idea	17
4	Mysteries	**Solved Mysteries**	Cause & Effect	21
5	People	**Technology Rivals**	Compare & Contrast	25
6	History	**Who Discovered America First?**	Categorizing	29
7	Culture	**The Haka, a Maori Tradition**	Main Idea	33
8	Jobs	**Subway Operators**	Sequencing	37
9	Earth Science	**Theories about the Earth**	Main Idea & Details	41
10	Culture	**Western Individuals, Eastern Groups**	Main Idea & Details	45

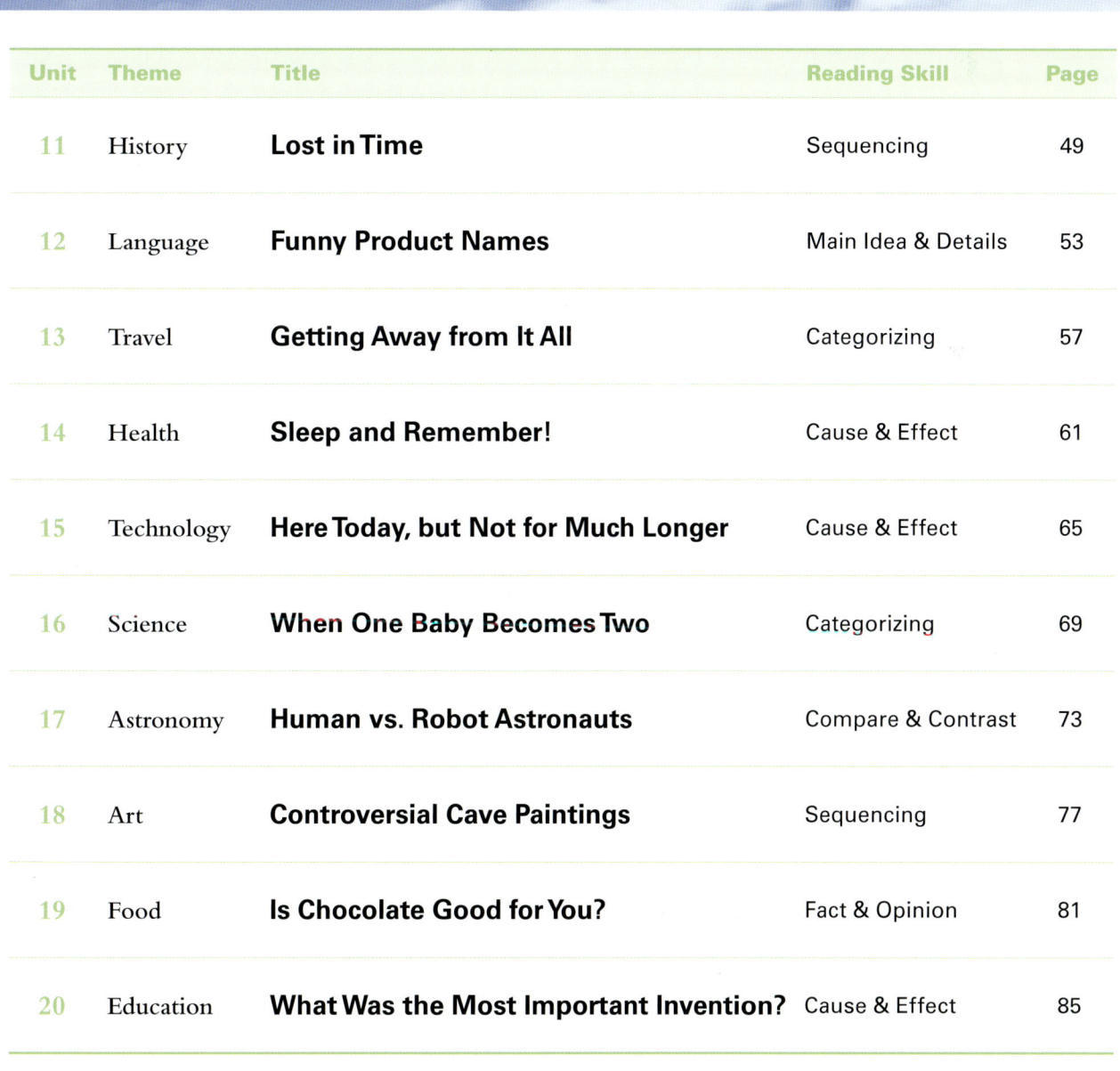

Unit	Theme	Title	Reading Skill	Page
11	History	**Lost in Time**	Sequencing	49
12	Language	**Funny Product Names**	Main Idea & Details	53
13	Travel	**Getting Away from It All**	Categorizing	57
14	Health	**Sleep and Remember!**	Cause & Effect	61
15	Technology	**Here Today, but Not for Much Longer**	Cause & Effect	65
16	Science	**When One Baby Becomes Two**	Categorizing	69
17	Astronomy	**Human vs. Robot Astronauts**	Compare & Contrast	73
18	Art	**Controversial Cave Paintings**	Sequencing	77
19	Food	**Is Chocolate Good for You?**	Fact & Opinion	81
20	Education	**What Was the Most Important Invention?**	Cause & Effect	85

Theme | *Places*
Reading Skill | *Sequencing*

Unit 1

Beautiful Trash

◂ Glass Beach in Fort Bragg, California

Before You Read

A **What do you know about garbage and recycling? Check *T* or *F*.**

1. People used to be allowed to throw away garbage in the oceans.   T / F
2. Nature cannot change human waste over time.   T / F
3. Trash can be reused in new and interesting ways.   T / F

B **Look at the vocabulary and check the ones you know.**

☐ handful   ☐ smooth   ☐ pound

☐ biodegradable   ☐ permit   ☐ go through with

Beautiful Trash

▶ *As you read, pay attention to how the glass changed over time.*

Have you ever seen a beach covered in pieces of glass? At one beach in Fort Bragg, California, you can. The beach is called Glass Beach. It is covered in thousands of tiny pieces of colorful glass. Glass Beach shows how nature can make our trash beautiful over time.

Glass Beach was created by accident. Beginning in 1906, people were **permitted** to throw away their garbage in the ocean near the city. People threw away glass bottles, appliances, and even cars. In 1967, the local government made it illegal to throw away trash in the water. After this, there were many cleanup efforts to recycle the metal and the other non-**biodegradable** waste. However, most of the glass had already been broken into tiny pieces. The glass was too difficult to remove, so it was left in the water. Over time, the pounding waves caused the rough pieces of glass to become **smooth**. These green, white, and brown pieces of smooth glass began washing up on shore, creating Glass Beach.

Today, thousands of people visit Glass Beach each year. Although there are rules against it, many visitors take home **handfuls** of the smooth glass beads. The city government has considered adding new glass to the beach. However, it still has not **gone through with** these plans. If you want to visit Glass Beach, you need to hurry before it disappears. Words 229

Vocabulary in Context

Write the words and phrases in bold next to their correct definitions.

1. _____ to allow something
2. _____ to officially accept or complete a plan
3. _____ an amount that you can hold in your hand
4. _____ having a flat, even surface; not having bumps
5. _____ capable of being broken down by natural processes

Reading Comprehension

1 What is the main idea of this passage?

   a. More people should recycle their trash.
   b. Nature turned our glass waste into something special.
   c. The Glass Beach is covered in trash and must be cleaned.
   d. People should stop taking the glass stones from Glass Beach.

2 What trash did the local government try to recycle?

   _____

3 Which is NOT true according to the passage?

   a. Glass Beach is covered in natural stones from the ocean.
   b. The waves pounded the glass into small, smooth pieces.
   c. The local government made it illegal to dump trash in the water.
   d. More glass still has not been added to Glass Beach by the government.

4 The glass waste was not removed from the water because _____.

   a. it is biodegradable
   b. it was too small to collect
   c. visitors like taking it home
   d. it was already on the beach

5 According to the passage, you can guess that _____.

   a. the glass on Glass Beach came from old bottles
   b. there are many glass beads left on Glass Beach
   c. most places still allow people to dump trash in the ocean
   d. the ocean can change all types of trash into something beautiful

Reading Skill *Sequencing is putting events in order from first to last. When we sequence, we can easily understand which events happen first, second, and so on.*

Fill in the chart and number the events in order.

Throwing away trash in the water became ❶_____.
People started to throw away ❷_____ in the ocean.
❸_____ pieces of glass started washing up on shore.
Visitors take handfuls of the smooth glass beads home so the city government considered ❹_____ new glass to the beach.
garbage   illegal   adding   smooth

Unit 1 11

Summary

Use the words and phrases in the box to complete the summary.

| handfuls | glass beads | rough | adding | threw away |

Glass Beach in California is a beach covered with thousands of ❶_____. The beads come from glass that people ❷_____ in the ocean. Over many years, the pounding waves turned the ❸_____ pieces of glass into smooth beads. The colorful beads washed up on the shore and made Glass Beach. Thousands of visitors go to Glass Beach every year and take home ❹_____ of glass beads. The city government is thinking of ❺_____ more glass to the beach, but still has not done so.

Vocabulary Expansion

A Match the words with their similar and opposite meanings from the box.

| allow | dump | even | keep | rough | ban |

Words	Similar Meaning	Opposite Meaning
smooth	_____	_____
permit	_____	_____
throw away	_____	_____

B Fill in the blanks using the words and phrases in bold from the passage. Change the forms if necessary.

1. He drew a _____ of candies from his pocket.
2. I can't believe how _____ the ice on the lake is.
3. You are not _____ to enter. You must leave now!
4. The city has decided to _____ its plan to build a new park.
5. Paper and food waste are _____, but glass and metal are not.

Theme | *Social Issues*
Reading Skill | *Fact & Opinion*

Unit 2

What Is a Geek?

Before You Read

A Check the statements that are true about you.

☐ 1. It is difficult for me to make friends and meet new people.
☐ 2. I enjoy watching only one or two types of movies, such as horror movies.
☐ 3. When new electronic devices such as smartphones come out, I want to learn all about them.

B Look at the vocabulary and check the ones you know.

☐ passionate   ☐ consider   ☐ horror
☐ social skills ☐ in general ☐ stereotype

What Is a Geek?

▸ *As you read, think about the different ways that a person can be considered a geek.*

Dear Jin-ho,

I'm very glad that you are enjoying your classes in America. In your last letter, you asked me what a geek was. Actually, it's funny that you ask. In high school, other students **considered** my friends and me to be geeks. I guess we were.

Geeks are usually defined as people who are really interested in new technology. They know more than most people about how computers work. Actually, geeks can be people who are really **passionate** about anything. For example, if someone really likes playing a certain game, that person can be called a geek. It doesn't matter if it's a computer game or not. Also, some people really like certain types of movies, like **horror** movies. They know almost everything about horror movies. Those people can also be called geeks.

Unfortunately, some people think that because geeks are really passionate about one thing, they don't have many **social skills**. A common **stereotype** about geeks is that they cannot talk about anything except the thing they are interested in. This makes it hard for them to make friends and get along with others in general. However, this isnet always true. I hope that answers your question.
Stay in touch,
Kate   Words 203

Vocabulary in Context
Write the words and phrases in bold next to their correct definitions.

1. _____ having strong feelings
2. _____ to think of as
3. _____ the ability to get along well with others
4. _____ a painful feeling caused by great shock or fear
5. _____ an unfair or untrue belief about a specific group of people

Reading Comprehension

1 **What is this passage mainly about?**

   a. how geeks are wonderful people
   b. why geeks have a hard time making friends
   c. the types of technology that geeks like the most
   d. what geeks are and how other people think of them

2 **What are two examples of things that geeks are passionate about in the passage?**

   _____

3 **Which is NOT true according to the passage?**

   a. Jinho was curious about what geeks were.
   b. Geeks know a lot about one specific subject.
   c. Geeks are only interested in new technology.
   d. Kate was considered to be a geek in high school.

4 **The most common stereotype about geeks is that they _____.**

   a. have excellent social skills
   b. only like to talk about one subject
   c. can get along with most people
   d. are only passionate about horror movies

5 **What can you learn about geeks from the passage?**

   a. All geeks love new machines.
   b. Some geeks have social skills.
   c. Computer geeks have no friends.
   d. Horror movie geeks are more outgoing than other geeks.

Reading Skill *A fact is a true statement that can be proven by evidence. An opinion is somebody's feelings about a subject. It may or may not be true.*

Write *F* for facts or *O* for opinions.

Statements	F or O
1. Anybody who is very passionate about any subject is a geek.	
2. Most geeks are good at playing computer games.	
3. Stereotypes about geeks can hurt their feelings.	
4. Some geeks have trouble getting along with other people.	

Summary

Use the words and phrases in the box to complete the summary.

geeks	interests	passionate	stereotypes	social skills

There are many types of ❶_____. Some are really ❷_____ about new technology and games while others are interested in different subjects like horror movies. Horror movie geeks know almost everything about horror movies. People believe many ❸_____ about geeks. For example, they may think that geeks have no ❹_____ or that they cannot talk about anything other than their ❺_____. Just like other stereotypes, this one is not always true.

Vocabulary Expansion

A Match the words with their similar meanings from the box.

typically	believe	enthusiastic

Words	Similar Meaning
passionate	_____
in general	_____
consider	_____

B Fill in the blanks using the words and phrases in bold from the passage. Change the forms if necessary.

1. Marco is really _____ about soccer, so he practices every day.
2. She is currently _____ to be the fastest woman in the world.
3. I can't watch _____ films. They just make me too uncomfortable.
4. The only way to develop your _____ is to go out and meet new people.
5. One _____ says that people who wear glasses are smart, but this isn't always true.

Theme | *Sports*
Reading Skill | *Main Idea*

Unit 3

Cheering for Cheerleaders

Before You Read

A Check the statements that you agree with.

☐ 1. Cheerleading is just for females.
☐ 2. Being a cheerleader can sometimes be dangerous.
☐ 3. Sports games are more exciting when there are cheerleaders.

B Look at the vocabulary and check the ones you know.

☐ stunt ☐ whip up ☐ appreciate
☐ out of shape ☐ squad ☐ responsibility

Cheering for Cheerleaders

▶ *As you read, think about the different jobs cheerleaders have.*

Matt is a cheerleader for his high school's football team. Although most people think cheerleaders are only females, many male students also help **whip up** support for their school's team.

One of Matt's **responsibilities** is to invent chants. An old, common chant goes like this: "Two-four-six-eight, who do we appreciate? Go Tigers!" Matt and his fellow cheerleaders try to create original and exciting chants to raise spirit for their team. Their football team is called the Titans. At their last game, Matt's cheerleading **squad** yelled, "We are the Titans / and we can't be beat / because we've got the power / to knock you off your feet!"

Matt's squad does not just brainstorm chants to yell at games. They also perform synchronized **stunts** such as the human pyramid, which is formed by ten cheerleaders. Matt and three of the other strongest cheerleaders line up side-by-side. Then they help three other cheerleaders climb up to stand on their shoulders. Then two more cheerleaders climb up to make a third row. The climax comes when a final cheerleader climbs all the way up to make a fourth row. Stunts like these require a lot of practice. They can be dangerous if someone is **out of shape** or has missed practice.

These days, cheerleading itself has become a sport. If you go to a game, cheer for the cheerleaders, too. **Words 228**

Vocabulary in Context
Write the words and phrases in bold next to their correct definitions.

1. _____ in poor physical condition
2. _____ a physical action showing skill
3. _____ something that is your job or duty to do
4. _____ a small group of people who work together
5. _____ to cause people to have strong feelings about something

Reading Comprehension

1 What is the main idea of this passage?

   a. Cheerleaders often perform exciting stunts.
   b. Men are not supposed to be cheerleaders.
   c. Cheerleading is a creative sport for both boys and girls.
   d. The main responsibility of cheerleaders is to invent new chants.

2 When is it dangerous to do stunts such as the human pyramid?

   _____

3 Which is true according to the passage?

   a. Cheerleaders only yell chants during games.
   b. The human pyramid in the passage is four rows high.
   c. At first, Matt's school did not accept the male cheerleaders.
   d. The human pyramid is performed by the four strongest cheerleaders.

4 What is NOT something that Matt's squad does?

   a. train to do difficult stunts
   b. try to attend every practice
   c. cheer for other cheerleaders
   d. invent creative chants to yell at games

5 According to the passage, you can guess that _____.

   a. there are more female cheerleaders than male cheerleaders
   b. cheerleaders learn how to catch and throw balls like other athletes
   c. Matt's cheerleading squad frequently uses the word "Tigers" in its chants
   d. Matt has never been in an accident while performing a stunt with his squad

Reading Skill *In most paragraphs, the main idea is usually the first sentence. It gives a general idea that is explained in the rest of the paragraph.*

Fill in the chart with the words in the box.

Paragraph 1	❶_____ students like Matt can be cheerleaders for their school teams.
Paragraph 2	Matt and the other cheerleaders create exciting ❷_____ to raise ❸_____.
Paragraph 3	Cheerleaders also perform synchronized ❹_____ such as the human pyramid.

| chants | stunts | male | team spirit |

Summary

Use the words in the box to complete the summary.

rows	sport	chants	squads	stunts

It is unusual for boys to be cheerleaders, but Matt is an example of many of the young men who join cheerleading ❶_____. Cheerleaders do not just come up with creative ❷_____. They also perform difficult ❸_____. An example is the human pyramid, which is formed by four ❹_____ of cheerleaders who stand on top of each others' shoulders. In this way, cheerleading has become a ❺_____ itself.

Vocabulary Expansion

A The suffix "-bility" is used to make some adjectives into nouns. Drop "-ble" and add "-bility" to the words in the box and match each word to a definition in the chart.

possible	responsible	acceptable

Words	Definition
_____	the state of being good enough
_____	something that it is your job or duty to do
_____	a chance that something might exist or be true

B Fill in the blanks using the words and phrases in bold from the passage. Change the forms if necessary.

1. I am part of the fire department's rescue _____.
2. Sarah is really _____ and needs to start exercising.
3. The _____ in this movie are amazing. They look so dangerous.
4. My main _____ is to create new dance moves for our team.
5. Our school held a performance to _____ support for the football team.

Theme | *Mysteries*
Reading Skill | *Cause & Effect*

Unit 4

Solved Mysteries

Before You Read

A Check the statements that you agree with.

☐ 1. Ghosts and monsters are real.
☐ 2. Most mysteries can never be solved.
☐ 3. Some events are caused by mysterious powers.

B Look at the vocabulary and check the ones you know.

☐ track ☐ solve ☐ slippery
☐ cursed ☐ baffle ☐ observation

Solved Mysteries

▸ *As you read, pay attention to what facts explain each of these mysteries.*

Everybody enjoys a good mystery. People love talking about Bigfoot or the Loch Ness Monster and wonder what they really are. It turns out, though, that many of these mysteries have already been solved. Here are two mysteries that are no longer a mystery.

The Bermuda Triangle is a triangle-shaped area of the Atlantic Ocean. It is located between Florida, Puerto Rico, and Bermuda. Some people believe that the area is **cursed** and that ships sailing through the Bermuda Triangle are likely to sink. This is true, just like the rest of the ocean. Because many ships travel through this part of the ocean, a high number of ships in total do sink. However, the percentage of ships that sink in the Bermuda Triangle is about the same as in the rest of the ocean.

Our next mystery comes from Death Valley, USA. The so-called "sailing stones" have **baffled** people for decades. These huge stones move across the land by themselves, leaving deep **tracks** in the ground. But they do not move by themselves. The area where the stones are sometimes floods. The flooding leaves the ground **slippery**. Strong winds in the area push the stones. This makes it seem like the stones move due to a mysterious power.

Reading about mysteries can be fun. However, almost all of them can be explained using science and **observation**. Words 227

Vocabulary in Context
Write the words in bold next to their correct definitions.

1. _____ to confuse someone completely
2. _____ the act of careful watching or listening
3. _____ affected by a mysterious power that causes bad things to happen
4. _____ difficult to stand or move on because of being smooth, wet, or icy
5. _____ a mark left in the ground by a moving person, animal, or vehicle

Reading Comprehension

1 What is this passage mainly about?

a. reasons that some mysteries cannot be solved
b. two famous mysteries that have not been solved
c. how flooding sometimes makes the land slippery
d. why science and observation can solve most mysteries

2 Where is the Bermuda Triangle located?

_____

3 Which is true according to the passage?

a. The sailing stones are pushed around by floodwaters.
b. People have known the cause of the sailing stones for decades.
c. The chance of ships sinking is nearly the same anywhere in the ocean.
d. Few ships pass through the Bermuda Triangle compared to other parts of the ocean.

4 The sailing stones move because _____.

a. the winds are strong
b. the ground is dry
c. they leave deep tracks
d. they have a mysterious power

5 According to the passage, you can guess that _____.

a. Death Valley has regular floods every year
b. there are reasonable and logical explanations for most mysteries
c. not many people have heard of Bigfoot or the Loch Ness Monster
d. areas where a large number of ships travel are usually more dangerous

Reading Skill   *Cause and effect is when one event causes something to happen. The cause explains why something happens, and the effect is what happens as a result.*

Fill in the chart with the words in the box.

Cause	Effect
Many ❶_____ travel through the Bermuda Triangle.	A high ❷_____ of ships in total sink there, but the ❸_____ is similar to other parts of the ocean.
Death Valley sometimes ❹_____ and has high winds.	The large stones in the valley ❺_____ across the ground.

| sail | floods | ships | percentage | number |

Unit 4 23

Summary

Use the words and phrases in the box to complete the summary.

| by themselves | science | pass through | slippery | number |

People enjoy reading about mysteries, but most of them can be solved using ❶_____ and observation. One such mystery is the Bermuda Triangle. A large ❷_____ of ships sink in this part of the ocean, but that is because many ships ❸_____ the area. Another mystery is the sailing stones of Death Valley. Many people think that these stones move ❹_____ across the ground. In fact, when the ground there becomes ❺_____, the high winds can push them.

Vocabulary Expansion

A Verbs that end in "-ve" can be changed into nouns by removing "-ve" and adding "-ution" or "-ation." They can be made into adjectives by removing the "-e" and adding "-able."

Verb	Noun	Adjective
solve	_____	_____
observe	_____	_____

B Fill in the blanks using the words in bold from the passage. Change the forms if necessary.

1. Be careful! The sidewalk is _____ when it snows.
2. People have been _____ by Bigfoot for several years.
3. I don't want to go into that house. I'm sure it's _____.
4. The hunters followed the deer's _____ to see where it went.
5. Scientists are trying to find the cause of the disease through careful _____.

Theme | *People*
Reading Skill | *Compare & Contrast*

Unit 5

Technology Rivals

Before You Read

A What do you know about Bill Gates and Steve Jobs? Guess and circle the answers.

1. They both (dropped out of / graduated from) university early.
2. (Bill Gates / Steve Jobs) created the company Microsoft.
3. One of Steve Jobs' most famous products is (Windows / the iPhone).

B Look at the vocabulary and check the ones you know.

☐ interface ☐ found ☐ revolutionize

☐ step down ☐ competitor ☐ operating system

Technology Rivals

▶ *As you read, pay attention to the ways that Bill Gates and Steve Jobs are similar and different.*

Two of the biggest business rivals in history are Bill Gates and Steve Jobs. Both of them left college early to **found** their own computer companies. Both were highly successful, creating products that millions of people use today. Gates and Jobs were serious **competitors**, but the two men had much in common.

Bill Gates left Harvard University in 1975. He and his friend Paul Allen started a new computer company, Microsoft. From the beginning, Gates focused on developing software, such as MS-DOS for IBM's new personal computers. In 1995, Bill Gates released Windows 95 and **revolutionized** the computing world. Today, almost every PC in the world uses some version of Windows. Bill Gates **stepped down** as CEO of Microsoft in 2000. However, he continues to manage certain parts of the company.

Like Bill Gates, Steve Jobs dropped out of college. Four years later in 1976, he founded Apple Computer with his friend Steve Wozniak to develop computer hardware. Apple was the first company to make the computer mouse popular. It also created the first personal computer with a graphical user **interface**, the Macintosh. Jobs was forced to leave Apple in 1985, but he returned in 1997. He then created a new type of computer, the iMac. After the success of the iMac, he created the iPod, iPhone, and the iPad. He remained CEO of Apple until his death in 2011. *Words 230*

Vocabulary in Context
Write the words and phrases in bold next to their correct definitions.

1. _____ to start an organization or a company
2. _____ to leave a job or official position; to resign
3. _____ to change something very much or completely
4. _____ a system that a person uses to control a computer
5. _____ someone who is trying to win or do better than others in sports or business

Reading Comprehension

1 What is this passage mainly about?

a. the ways that two big competitors' lives were similar
b. how Bill Gates became more successful than Steve Jobs
c. the strategies that Bill Gates and Steve Jobs used to succeed
d. reasons that Apple's products are some of the most popular today

2 How did Bill Gates revolutionize the computer world?

_____

3 Which is true according to the passage?

a. Steve Jobs dropped out of college in 1976.
b. Bill Gates eventually graduated from Harvard.
c. Apple released many new products after 1997.
d. Microsoft was founded by Bill Gates and his brother.

4 Which is NOT mentioned as a similarity between Bill Gates and Steve Jobs?

a. They dropped out of college.
b. They founded a computer company.
c. They developed computer software.
d. They made products loved by many people.

5 According to the passage, what can you guess about Bill Gates?

a. He developed the first home computer.
b. He mainly wanted to develop new hardware.
c. He was embarrassed that he did not finish college.
d. He designed computer programs that are still used today.

Reading Skill *Comparing and contrasting is a way to explain how two or more things are similar and different.*

Fill in the chart with the words in the box.

Bill Gates	Steve Jobs
• He ❶_____ of Harvard to found Microsoft.	• He ❹_____ Apple after dropping out of college.
• He focused on developing ❷_____ like Windows.	• He developed ❺_____ such as the Macintosh computer.
• He still ❸_____ parts of Microsoft.	• He remained CEO until his death in 2011.

| manages | hardware | founded | dropped out | software |

Unit 5 27

Summary

Use the words and phrases in the box to complete the summary.

hardware	stepped down	Macintosh	dropped out	developed

Bill Gates and Steve Jobs were serious rivals. The main way they were similar was they both ❶_____ of college and founded computer companies. Bill Gates' company Microsoft mostly ❷_____ software such as MS-DOS and Windows. On the other hand, Steve Jobs' company Apple focused on creating ❸_____. The company made the first popular computer mouse and the ❹_____ personal computer. While they were both CEOs, Gates ❺_____ from his position. But Jobs worked as CEO of Apple until his death.

Vocabulary Expansion

A Match the words and phrases with their similar meanings from the box.

resign	create	rival

Words	Similar Meaning
found	_____
competitor	_____
step down	_____

B Fill in the blanks using the words and phrases in bold from the passage. Change the forms if necessary.

1. This company was _____ in 1892.
2. I love the new _____ on this computer. It's so easy to use.
3. Communication was _____ with the development of the Internet.
4. The governor _____ after people found out he stole tax money.
5. Apple and Samsung are the two main _____ in the cell phone market.

Theme | *History*
Reading Skill | *Categorizing*

Unit 6

Who Discovered America First?

◀ Columbus statue in the Dominican Republic

Before You Read

A What do you know about Christopher Columbus? Guess and circle the answers.

He was an (American / Italian) explorer.
He is believed to discover (America / Asia).

B Look at the vocabulary and check the ones you know.

- ☐ explorer
- ☐ spread
- ☐ evidence
- ☐ introduce
- ☐ discover
- ☐ all the way

Who Discovered America First?

▸ *As you read, focus on who discovered America.*

Say this sentence out loud: "In 1492, Christopher Columbus sailed the ocean blue." Many young American students use this sentence to remember when Columbus **discovered** America. The students learn that Columbus came to America before anyone else. However, was Columbus really the first person to discover America?

Many researchers believe that East Asians were the first people to reach America. They crossed an ice bridge from eastern Russia to Alaska thousands of years ago. After this ice bridge melted, they could not go back to Asia. These **explorers** became the American Indians. They and their children spread south. They went all the way down through Central America into South America.

In addition, other Europeans found North America before Columbus. In 938 A.D., some Vikings sailed to Greenland. They made villages there. A few of these Vikings continued to sail west. They made it to the east coast of what is now Canada. There is still some **evidence** of Viking camps along the Canadian coast.

We can see that Columbus was not the first person to "discover" America. Other brave explorers had already found these lands. Many made their homes there. However, we can say that Columbus **introduced** the Americas to Europe. He was the first to **spread** this news to all Europeans. Words 212

Vocabulary in Context   *Write the words in bold next to their correct definitions.*

1. _____ to distribute
2. _____ a clue or sign of something
3. _____ to find a place for the first time
4. _____ to show something new to others
5. _____ a person who travels to places to find something

Reading Comprehension

1. **What is the main idea of this passage?**

   a. The Vikings were famous explorers.
   b. American Indians are relatives of East Asians.
   c. An ice bridge once connected Asia to America.
   d. Columbus was not the first to discover America.

2. **How far did the American Indians explore?**

   a. into North America
   b. to Alaska
   c. into South America
   d. to the Canadian coast

3. **How do we know that Vikings once lived in America?**

   _____

4. **Which is true according to the passage?**

   a. Columbus sailed in 938 A.D.
   b. East Asians became the American Indians.
   c. The Vikings crossed an ice bridge to get to Canada.
   d. Columbus discovered North America for the first time.

5. **What can you guess about the early East Asians?**

   a. They sometimes fought with the Vikings.
   b. They could return to Asia whenever they wanted.
   c. They met and made friends with the American Indians.
   d. They did not have the technology to make ships to go to Asia.

Reading Skill *Categorizing information means to arrange information or items into different groups.*

Fill in the chart with the words in the box.

Discoverers of America	
East Asians	crossed an ice ❶_____ between Russia and Alaska and became American ❷_____
❸_____	sailed to Greenland in 938 and made it to Canada later
Christopher Columbus	• was not the first person to ❹_____ America • was the first to ❺_____ the Americas to Europe

| Vikings | discover | introduce | Indians | bridge |

Summary

Use the words and phrases in the box to complete the summary.

| ice bridge | East Asians | Vikings | true | introduce |

Although many American students learn that Christopher Columbus "discovered" America, this is not exactly ❶_____. Researchers believe the first people to discover America were ❷_____. They crossed an ancient ❸_____ between Asia and Alaska. These people and their children became the American Indians. The next group to discover America was the ❹_____. However, they did not tell other Europeans about America. The first to ❺_____ America to Europe was Christopher Columbus.

Vocabulary Expansion

A Match the words with their similar and opposite meanings from the box.

| keep | forget | find | miss | stop | recall |

Words	Similar Meaning	Opposite Meaning
discover	_____	_____
continue	_____	_____
remember	_____	_____

B Fill in the blanks using the words in bold from the passage. Change the forms if necessary.

1. Marco Polo was a famous Italian _____.

2. Cindy, I want to _____ you to my friend Bill.

3. The police could not _____ who had taken the girl's bicycle.

4. It's not a good idea to _____ rumors because they could be false.

5. When you write an essay, you need clear _____ to support your arguments.

Theme | *Culture*
Reading Skill | *Main Idea*

Unit 7

The Haka, a Maori Tradition

Before You Read

A What do you know about the haka? Guess and circle the answers.

1. The haka is originally from (New Zealand / the United Kingdom).
2. It is a traditional type of (music / dance).
3. It was usually used before (weddings / wars) by groups of people.

B Look at the vocabulary and check the ones you know.

☐ discourage ☐ slap ☐ achievement

☐ poke out ☐ enemy ☐ individually

The Haka, a Maori Tradition

▶ *As you read, think of the different ways people used the haka.*

If you have ever watched the All Blacks rugby team, then you have seen the haka. The haka is a traditional Maori dance. It is performed by a group. The dancers move and shout in rhythm. They also stamp their feet and **slap** their arms. Sometimes, dancers show the whites of their eyes and **poke out** their tongues.

Many different forms of the haka exist. One type is *peruperu*. This was performed before a battle to **discourage** the enemy. To do the *peruperu*, the dancer must jump while keeping their legs under their lower body. Another type of haka is the *ngeri*. In this dance, each performer moves individually to express their feelings. Its purpose was to help the warriors prepare mentally for battle.

Since 1905, the New Zealand rugby team has performed the haka. This has helped popularize the dance. But it has also led to some misunderstandings. Many believe that the haka was used only by men. They think it was a war dance to frighten **enemies**. In reality, men, women, and even children performed the haka for many reasons. The haka was used to welcome respected guests or to celebrate special **achievements**. When people died, their villages would perform the haka at their funeral.

The haka is an important cultural tradition for the Maori people. Thanks to the All Blacks, the haka will remain popular for many years to come.   Words 233

Vocabulary in Context

Write the words and phrases in bold next to their correct definitions.

1. _____ something that results from hard work
2. _____ to make someone less hopeful or confident
3. _____ a group of people you fight against in a war
4. _____ to stick out something so that part of it can be seen
5. _____ to hit something with the front or back of your hand

Reading Comprehension

1 **What is the main idea of this passage?**

a. Only men should perform the haka dance.
b. There are many different types of haka dances.
c. The All Blacks team is famous for performing the haka.
d. The haka is a traditional dance that is still popular today.

2 **Which is true about the *ngeri* dance according to the passage?**

a. It requires each dancer to move on their own.
b. It was used while the warriors fought battles.
c. It helped warriors to prepare physically for battle.
d. It requires dancers to keep their legs beneath their lower body.

3 **What is one misunderstanding about the haka?**

One misunderstanding is that it _____.

4 **Which is NOT a reason the haka is performed?**

a. to celebrate a great achievement
b. to show respect to visitors
c. to have a party after winning a battle
d. to honor someone at their funeral

5 **According to the passage, you can guess that _____.**

a. Maori people no longer perform the haka
b. the haka is usually performed by individuals
c. people do not make noise while performing the haka
d. not many people knew about the haka before 1905

Reading Skill *In most paragraphs, the main idea is usually the first sentence. It gives a general idea that is explained in the rest of the paragraph.*

Fill in the chart with the words in the box.

Paragraph 1	The haka is a ❶_____ Maori dance.
Paragraph 2	There are many ❷_____ types of haka dances including *peruperu* and *ngeri*.
Paragraph 3	The All Blacks made the haka ❸_____ but also created some ❹_____ about it.

| different | misunderstandings | popular | traditional |

Unit 7 35

Summary

Use the words in the box to complete the summary.

war dance   achievements   everybody   tradition   stamping

The haka is a traditional dance of New Zealand. The All Blacks made the dance popular, but it was a Maori ❶_____ long before that. To perform the haka, dancers must move in rhythm, ❷_____ their feet and shouting. One type of the haka is the *peruperu*, and another type is the *ngeri*. Some people believe that the haka was a ❸_____ used only by men. The truth is ❹_____ performed the haka for many reasons. Some of the reasons include welcoming visitors and celebrating ❺_____.

Vocabulary Expansion

A Many verbs that end in "-e" can be changed into nouns by adding "-ment." They can be made into adjectives by removing the "-e" and adding "-ing." Change the verbs into nouns and adjectives.

Verb	Noun	Adjective
achieve	_____	_____
require	_____	_____
discourage	_____	_____

B Fill in the blanks using the words and phrases in bold from the passage. Change the forms if necessary.

1. Your toe is _____ of a hole in your sock.
2. Diana _____ Andy's face for saying something rude.
3. The United States and Russia were _____ for many years.
4. My greatest _____ in life was becoming the school president.
5. I don't want to _____ you, but your singing is not very good.

Theme | *Jobs*
Reading Skill | *Sequencing*

Unit 8

Subway Operators

Before You Read

A **How much do you know about subway operators? Check *T* or *F*.**

1. The only job of a subway operator is driving the trains.   T / F
2. Subway operators have to know a lot of safety rules.   T / F
3. People who want to be subway operators must pass a test.   T / F

B **Look at the vocabulary and check the ones you know.**

☐ extensive ☐ candidate ☐ procedure
☐ operate ☐ emergency ☐ be on the lookout

Unit 8 37

Subway Operators

▶ *As you read, think of all the different jobs a subway operator must do.*

You might think that a computer controls most subway trains. The fact is that most trains are controlled by subway operators. Driving a huge subway train may sound like fun. However, being a subway operator is a very difficult and stressful job.

To become a subway operator, **candidates** first must complete an extensive training program. These programs can last up to six months. Applicants learn how to **operate** different types of trains. They also receive training for **emergencies**. For instance, they learn what to do when there is a stopped train ahead. After the training is done, candidates must pass written exams. These exams test the candidates on operational and safety **procedures**. Candidates who fail these exams cannot become operators.

Once they pass the exam, candidates are ready to become subway operators. The main responsibility of an operator is driving the trains. They must also open and close the train doors and make sure the passengers are safe. Sometimes people fall onto the tracks. So drivers must always **be on the lookout** and be ready to stop the train quickly. Otherwise, accidents can occur.

Being a subway operator can be an exciting job. It can also be a stressful job. Operators must always pay attention to make sure everyone is safe.   Words 211

Vocabulary in Context
Write the words and phrases in bold next to their correct definitions.

1. _____ to cause to work or be in action
2. _____ the usual way of doing something
3. _____ an unexpected and dangerous situation
4. _____ a person who is being considered for a job
5. _____ to watch carefully for something to avoid danger, etc.

Reading Comprehension

1 **What is the main idea of this passage?**

a. Being a subway operator is a relaxing job.
b. Working as a subway operator can be challenging.
c. The training program to be an operator lasts a long time.
d. Subway operator is one of the most popular jobs today.

2 **What do the candidates have to do first to become a subway operator?**

_____

3 **Which is true about the training program?**

a. It lasts over six months.
b. It includes a printed exam.
c. It trains candidates how to prevent emergencies.
d. It teaches applicants how to drive one type of train.

4 **What is NOT mentioned as a responsibility of a subway operator?**

a. making announcements
b. driving the trains
c. opening and closing the doors
d. keeping the passengers safe

5 **According to the passage, you can guess that _____.**

a. people sometimes get hurt on the subway
b. there has never been a subway accident
c. working as a subway operator releases stress
d. most subway operators quit their jobs after a short time

Reading Skill *Sequencing is putting events in order from first to last. When we sequence, we can easily understand which events happen first, second, and so on.*

Fill in the chart and number the events in order.

How to Become a Subway Operator
Candidates are also taught what to do in an ❶_____.
Applicants then take a ❷_____ exam.
Candidates learn how to drive ❸_____ types of trains.
Once they ❹_____ the exam, applicants can work as an operator.
different   emergency   pass   written

Unit 8 39

Summary

Use the words in the box to complete the summary.

exam	stressful	stop	responsibilities	extensive

Working as a subway operator can be a fun but ❶_____ job. First, candidates need to complete an ❷_____ training program. They must learn how to drive many types of trains and what to do in an emergency. After the training, candidates must pass a written ❸_____. Once they begin working as an operator, their main ❹_____ include driving the trains and making sure the passengers are safe. If someone falls on the tracks, the operators need to be ready to ❺_____ the trains quickly.

Vocabulary Expansion

A Match the words with their similar meanings from the box.

control	broad	process

Words	Similar Meaning
procedure	_____
operate	_____
extensive	_____

B Fill in the blanks using the words and phrases in bold from the passage. Change the forms if necessary.

1. I'm always _____ for sales at grocery stores.

2. It was a simple _____ to change the clock batteries.

3. Read the manual before you _____ the machine.

4. Do you know what to do when there is a fire or another _____?

5. Over 50 _____ have applied for this job. It will be hard to choose just one.

Theme | *Earth Science*
Reading Skill | *Main Idea & Details*

Unit 9

Theories about the Earth

Before You Read

A How much do you know about the Earth? Check *T* or *F*.

1. The inside of the Earth is very cold.   T / F
2. Our Earth is made up of continents and oceans.   T / F
3. The continents have been moving slowly for millions of years.   T / F

B Look at the vocabulary and check the ones you know.

☐ disprove   ☐ geologist   ☐ solid
☐ continent ☐ theory   ☐ complex

Theories about the Earth

▶ *As you read, pay attention to how scientists' theories about the Earth have changed over time.*

Reporter	Today, we are interviewing Robert James, a famous **geologist**. Robert, do geologists know everything there is to know about the Earth?
Robert James	Absolutely not. The Earth is so **complex** that it will take a long time to learn all of its secrets. Also, our ideas about the Earth today may completely change with new discoveries.
Reporter	What do you mean by that?
Robert James	For example, before 1912, geologists thought the mountains and **continents** of the Earth did not move. They thought the Earth was a **solid** ball of hard rock. Then, in 1912, a geologist named Alfred Wegener said this was not true. He said the inside of the Earth was so hot that rocks melted. He thought the continents floated on this mass of liquid rock and have been moving slowly for millions of years. At first, most scientists laughed at his ideas, but later observations proved that Wegener was right.
Reporter	So geologists are not always right?
Robert James	All scientists observe the environment. From these observations, we can make theories. But if someone finds a new method to make better observations, that person may find evidence that **disproves** earlier guesses. Then we should change our ideas to fit the new evidence. That is what science is all about. **Words 214**

Vocabulary in Context   *Write the words in bold next to their correct definitions.*

1. _____ difficult to understand
2. _____ a very large land mass
3. _____ a scientist who studies the Earth
4. _____ having no space inside; firm or hard
5. _____ to show that something is wrong or false

Reading Comprehension

1 What is this passage mainly about?

   a. what the inside of the Earth is made of
   b. how scientists have been wrong in the past
   c. why our knowledge about the Earth is always changing
   d. why Alfred Wegener was ignored by other scientists at first

2 Why did geologists before 1912 believe that the continents did not move?

   _____

3 Which is NOT true according to the passage?

   a. The inside of the Earth is hard rock.
   b. The continents are always moving slowly.
   c. Scientists are still learning about the Earth.
   d. Current theories about geology may change in the future.

4 Why is it impossible for scientists to say that their theories are always correct?

   a. Every scientist makes different observations.
   b. Once a theory is made, it cannot be changed.
   c. Scientific beliefs can change based on new evidence.
   d. There is no evidence to support the original theories.

5 According to the passage, you can guess that _____.

   a. the Earth is cooling rapidly
   b. scientists usually believe new theories right away
   c. the ocean floor is a very hot and dangerous place
   d. the shape of the continents was different a long time ago

Reading Skill *The main idea is usually at the beginning of a text and makes a general statement. The supporting details are specific ideas that support the main idea.*

Fill in the chart with the words in the box.

Main Idea	Geologists' ❶_____ about the Earth are always changing.
Details	• Scientists thought the land on the Earth did not ❷_____. • Alfred Wegener said the inside of the Earth was a mass of ❸_____ and that the ❹_____ have moved slowly for millions of years.

move	liquid rock	theories	continents

Summary

Use the words in the box to complete the summary.

theories	evidence	geologists	complex	observations

❶_____ are still learning new things about the Earth because it is so ❷_____. Also, scientists admit that their theories are based on incomplete evidence. Newer and better ways of observing the Earth are always being discovered. These new ❸_____ may lead to new evidence that can change existing ❹_____. For instance, Alfred Wegener believed the inside of the Earth was liquid rock and that the continents have moved slowly for millions of years. Eventually, other scientists accepted Wegener's ❺_____ and changed their ideas.

Vocabulary Expansion

A The prefix "dis-" means "to do the opposite" or "not." Add "dis-" to the words in the box and match each word to a definition in the chart.

connect	prove	appear

Words	Definition
_____	to stop being seen
_____	to show that something is false or wrong
_____	to separate from something else

B Fill in the blanks using the words in bold from the passage. Change the forms if necessary.

1. A _____ can tell us about the Earth.
2. Stone is a _____ material, but water is not.
3. The lake is located in the southern part of the _____.
4. This subway map is too _____. I can't understand it.
5. The lawyer presented evidence to _____ the opponent's argument.

Theme | *Culture*
Reading Skill | *Main Idea & Details*

Unit 10

Western Individuals, Eastern Groups

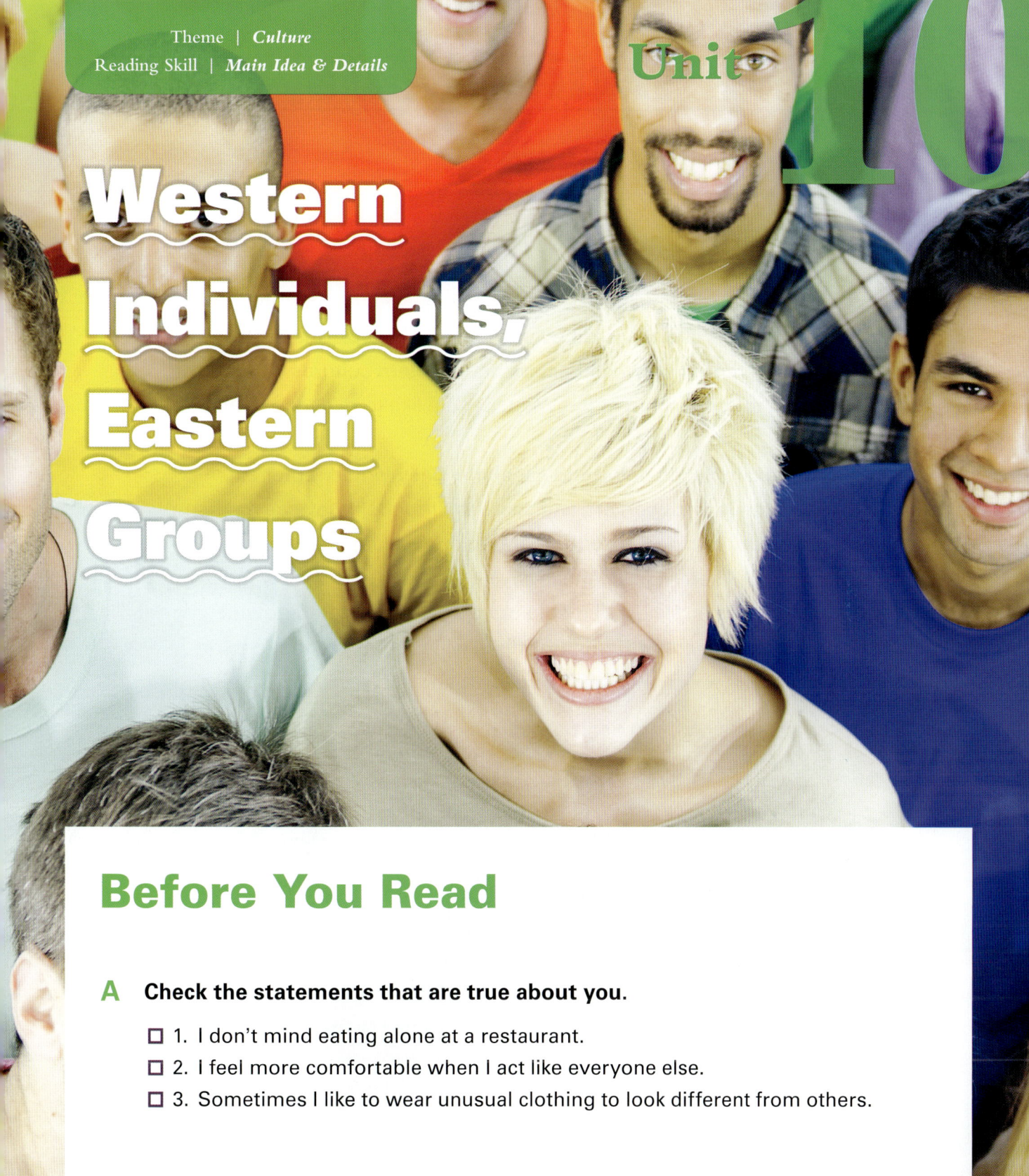

Before You Read

A Check the statements that are true about you.

☐ 1. I don't mind eating alone at a restaurant.
☐ 2. I feel more comfortable when I act like everyone else.
☐ 3. Sometimes I like to wear unusual clothing to look different from others.

B Look at the vocabulary and check the ones you know.

☐ globalized   ☐ pity   ☐ express
☐ highlight   ☐ conform   ☐ approach

Western Individuals, Eastern Groups

▶ *As you read, compare how Westerners and Easterners behave differently.*

Many Asians think it is unusual to do things alone. On the other hand, many Westerners think it is strange to do everything as a group. This **highlights** one of the biggest differences between Eastern and Western cultures. In the East, people like to belong to groups, but in the West, people like to **express** their individuality.

Koreans, for example, do not like to eat alone. They would rather eat together with their friends or coworkers and share their food. If they see a person who is eating alone, they may feel **pity** for that person. The Japanese also like to do things as a group. There is a Japanese saying about people who want to be different. The saying is, "The nail that sticks up gets hammered down." This means that if someone acts differently, others will try to make that person **conform** and act like everyone else.

On the other hand, many Westerners prefer to do some things alone. Many like to get away from their coworkers to have lunch with only a newspaper or a good book for company. Westerners seem to need their own space more often.

Neither style is basically good or bad. They just show differences in culture. In our **globalized** world, it is important to understand these different cultural approaches to life.   Words 219

Vocabulary in Context
Write the words in bold next to their correct definitions.

1. _____ to mark or emphasize something
2. _____ a feeling of sorrow for someone else
3. _____ involving or affecting the entire world
4. _____ to communicate by words or behavior
5. _____ to change oneself to be similar to society

Reading Comprehension

1 What is the main idea of this passage?

   a. When in Rome, do as the Romans do.
   b. Asians and Westerners have different eating habits.
   c. Each country in the world has its own valuable culture.
   d. Easterners and Westerners think differently about being alone or in a group.

2 What does the saying, "The nail that sticks up gets hammered down," mean?

   It means people will try to make someone who _____.

3 Which is NOT true according to the passage?

   a. It is important to conform in Japanese society.
   b. The Western approach of expressing individuality is rude.
   c. Koreans usually feel pity for someone who is eating alone.
   d. Westerners sometimes eat a meal with a book or newspaper.

4 Westerners like to eat meals alone because they _____.

   a. do not like their coworkers   b. want time to themselves
   c. enjoy reading more than talking   d. do not have much time to eat

5 According to the passage, you can guess that _____.

   a. a Westerner who eats alone has no friends
   b. Japanese and Korean approaches to life are similar
   c. Westerners do not like to see people who do not conform to society
   d. Japanese and Western lifestyles are more alike than Japanese and Korean lifestyles

<u>**Reading Skill**</u> *The main idea is usually at the beginning of a text and makes a general statement. The supporting details are specific ideas that support the main idea.*

Fill in the chart with the words in the box.

Main Idea	Asians prefer to do things as a ❶_____, while Westerners sometimes prefer to do things as ❷_____.
Details	• Koreans often eat together and feel ❸_____ for people eating alone. • Japanese people dislike people who act ❹_____. • Westerners will ❺_____ from their coworkers to eat alone and read a newspaper or a book.

pity   group   individuals   get away   differently

Unit 10 **47**

Summary

Use the words in the box to complete the summary.

| personal | differences | approach | conformity | groups |

One of the biggest ❶_____ between Eastern and Western cultures is how people spend their free time. Traditionally, Easterners like to do things in ❷_____ whereas Westerners spend more time alone. For example, Easterners tend to think that group activities and ❸_____ are more important. Westerners will eat by themselves to catch up on some reading or to enjoy some ❹_____ time alone. Neither ❺_____ is good or bad; they are just different.

Vocabulary Expansion

A Match the words with their similar meanings from the box.

| show | obey | emphasize |

Words	Similar Meaning
conform	_____
highlight	_____
express	_____

B Fill in the blanks using the words in bold from the passage. Change the forms if necessary.

1. It's a _____ that you can't come on the trip with us.
2. All students must _____ to the rules of this school.
3. Jacqueline wears unusual clothing to _____ her creativity.
4. Today, the world is so _____ that you can get a taco in Tokyo.
5. The principal's speech _____ the importance of staying in school.

Theme | *History*
Reading Skill | *Sequencing*

Unit 11

Lost in Time

Neanderthal man ▶

Before You Read

A How much do you know about Neanderthals? Check *T* or *F*.

1. They probably lived thousands of years ago.   T / F
2. They lived in America and Africa.   T / F
3. They were taller than modern humans are.   T / F

B Look at the vocabulary and check the ones you know.

- ☐ odd
- ☐ die out
- ☐ alongside
- ☐ curved
- ☐ muscular
- ☐ deformed

Unit 11 49

Lost in Time

▶ *As you read, focus on the order of the events and the characteristics of Neanderthals.*

My name is *Lost in Time*. I died 40,000 years ago in a cave along a valley. This valley, called Neanderthal, is in Germany. My bones were discovered by miners in 1856. Scientists examined my bones and found them odd. They were thicker and more **curved** than normal human bones.

At first, scientists thought I was a **deformed** man. However, a few years later, an Irish scientist named William King guessed the truth. King had read Charles Darwin's famous book on evolution. Because of this book, King guessed correctly that I was an ancient relative of modern humans. He called me Neanderthal man because of where my bones were found. Since then, bones from other Neanderthals have been discovered in Europe and central Asia.

Scientists did tests on these bones. The results show humans like me lived between 200,000 and 30,000 years ago. We lived during the most recent Ice Age and lived longer than *Homo sapiens*, or modern humans, have lived on Earth. If you saw me today, you would think I was a little short but very strong. My chest, neck, head, and especially my arms would be bigger and more **muscular** than normal.

When *Homo sapiens* came out of Africa, they moved into my lands. We lived **alongside** them for thousands of years until the last of us **died out**. All that remains is our bones. Words 229

Vocabulary in Context
Write the words and phrases in bold next to their correct definitions.

1. _____ not straight
2. _____ to disappear completely
3. _____ shaped in an unusual way
4. _____ having large strong muscles
5. _____ at the same time as something else

Reading Comprehension

1 What is the main idea of this passage?

  a. Neanderthals were ancient human relatives.
  b. All creatures evolved from a common ancestor.
  c. Neanderthals were much stronger than modern humans are.
  d. Charles Darwin's book proved that there were no Neanderthals.

2 Who was the first to discover the Neanderthal man?

  _____

3 Where did modern humans come from?

  a. Asia   b. Africa   c. Australia   d. the Middle East

4 Which is NOT true about Neanderthals?

  a. Their bones were found in Asia and Europe.
  b. They lived longer than modern humans have.
  c. They were shorter and stronger than modern humans.
  d. They were named after the people who found their bones.

5 According to the passage, what can you guess about the Neanderthals?

  a. Neanderthals liked living in cold climates.
  b. Most Neanderthals had more children than most humans have.
  c. Human beings and Neanderthals fought wars with each other.
  d. The Neanderthals did not leave behind much evidence of their culture.

Reading Skill *Sequencing is putting events in order from first to last. When we sequence, we can easily understand which events happen first, second, and so on.*

Fill in the chart and number the events in order.

Scientists ❶_____ the bones and thought they were strange.
More bones were found in ❷_____ and Asia.
❸_____ discovered bones in a valley.
One scientist guessed the bones belonged to an ❹_____.

early human	miners	examined	Europe

Unit 11 51

Summary

Use the words in the box to complete the summary.

| deformed | guessed | idea | bones | discoveries |

When Neanderthal ❶_____ were first discovered in Germany, nobody knew what they were. Most scientists just said they were from a ❷_____ human being. However, an Irish scientist named William King used Darwin's book about evolution to make a different guess. He ❸_____ that the bones were from an early type of human. His ❹_____ was proven correct by later ❺_____ of similar bones in Europe and Asia.

Vocabulary Expansion

A Match the words with their similar meanings from the box.

| rounded | together with | strange |

Words	Similar Meaning
odd	_____
curved	_____
alongside	_____

B Fill in the blanks using the words and phrases in bold from the passage. Change the forms if necessary.

1. If there is no land for tigers to live in, they will _____.
2. Alex is very _____ since he exercises a lot at the gym.
3. I cannot work _____ my sister because we always fight.
4. My bicycle has _____ handlebars instead of straight ones.
5. The firefighter's face is _____ since he had an accident.

Theme | *Language*
Reading Skill | *Main Idea & Details*

Unit 12

Funny Product Names

Before You Read

A Check the statements that you agree with.

☐ 1. Pocari Sweat is a strange name for a drink.
☐ 2. Product names sometimes sound silly in foreign languages.
☐ 3. Companies should change their product names when they sell their products in foreign countries.

B Look at the vocabulary and check the ones you know.

☐ gross   ☐ sweat   ☐ character
☐ disgust   ☐ grave   ☐ mistranslate

Funny Product Names

▶ *As you read, think about the ways a product's name can sound strange to people from other countries.*

Dear Jim,

    I have a funny story to tell you. I brought a can of Pocari Sweat to my middle school in Los Angeles. There is a Japanese store in my neighborhood that sells it. Anyway, when I took it out of my lunchbox, my American friends looked at it with **disgust**. "Who is Pocari," they asked, "and why would you want to drink his **sweat**?" I didn't realize it, but the name sounds **gross** to many Americans. They don't want to drink something with the word "sweat" in the name. To them, it sounds like the can contains sweat from some guy named Pocari! Isn't that funny?

Dear Yuri,

    That is a funny story. You would be surprised by how some product names are **mistranslated** in different languages. An American pizza restaurant tried to sell calzones to Spanish speakers. However, the restaurant didn't know that "calzone" means "underwear" in Spanish. Imagine walking into a restaurant and ordering pepperoni underwear for lunch! Even big companies have trouble in foreign countries. When Coca-Cola was first introduced in China, it was spelled with Chinese **characters** to make the sound "ke-kou-ke-la." Those Chinese characters translated as "bite the wax tadpole," which makes no sense at all. Pepsi's slogan "Come alive with the Pepsi Generation" was translated into Chinese as "Pepsi brings your ancestors back from the grave." Words 224

Vocabulary in Context
Write the words in bold next to their correct definitions.

1. _____ very unpleasant
2. _____ a feeling of strong dislike
3. _____ a printed or written letter or symbol
4. _____ the liquid that is on your skin when you are hot
5. _____ to change words from one language into another incorrectly

Reading Comprehension

1 What is the main idea of this passage?

   a. Pocari Sweat is an international brand name that is very successful.

   b. Some brand names become funny when translated into other languages.

   c. Companies need to be careful before translating their slogans into Chinese.

   d. There is no safe way to translate a brand name into all the languages of the world.

2 Why do Yuri's American friends ask "Who is Pocari?"

   _____

3 What does "calzone" mean in Spanish?

   a. lunchbox   b. skirt   c. tadpole   d. underwear

4 Which is true according to the passage?

   a. Pepsi's slogan was changed for the Chinese market.

   b. Yuri's friends gave her Pocari Sweat to drink for lunch.

   c. Americans like the word "sweat" on something they will drink.

   d. Coca-Cola's brand name made no sense when translated into Chinese.

5 According to the passage, what can you guess about big companies?

   a. They use funny tricks to make their products popular.

   b. They are always insensitive to the cultures in other countries.

   c. They like to make strange mistranslations of their brand names or slogans.

   d. They need to consult with native speakers before translating advertisements.

Reading Skill *The main idea is usually at the beginning of a text and makes a general statement. The supporting details are specific ideas that support the main idea.*

Fill in the chart with the words in the box.

Main Idea	Product names can sound strange or be ❶_____ into foreign languages.
Details	• The name Pocari Sweat sounds ❷_____ to many Americans. • Calzone means ❸_____ in Spanish. • The Chinese ❹_____ translate Coca-Cola as "bite the wax tadpole." • Pepsi's slogan was translated into Chinese as "Pepsi brings your ❺_____ back from the grave."

| ancestors | characters | mistranslated | disgusting | underwear |

Unit 12 55

Summary

Use the words in the box to complete the summary.

| Spanish | slogans | translates | grave | sweat |

Some product names or advertising ❶_____ can have funny meanings when they are translated into other languages. For example, many Americans may not like the sound of "Pocari Sweat." It sounds like it is ❷_____ from some person whose name is Pocari. Another example is the Italian dish called "calzone." It means "underwear" in ❸_____. If you spell the name Coca-Cola in Chinese characters, the name ❹_____ into "bite the wax tadpole." Pepsi's slogan promised to bring Chinese people's ancestors back from the ❺_____.

Vocabulary Expansion

A The prefix "mis-" means "wrong", "bad," or "mistaken." Add "mis-" to the words in the box and match each word to a definition in the chart.

| lead | translate | understand |

Words	Definition
_____	to not understand correctly
_____	to bring in the wrong direction
_____	to change from one language to another wrongly

B Fill in the blanks using the words in bold from the passage. Change the forms if necessary.

1. Chinese and Japanese _____ look similar.
2. Julie looked away in _____ as her brother ate a bug.
3. Your behavior is _____. You shouldn't act that way.
4. Carry a small towel to wipe off your _____ during the summer.
5. A lot of people were upset when the company _____ the name of its product.

Theme | *Travel*
Reading Skill | *Categorizing*

Unit **13**

Getting Away from It All

◀ Moai stone statues at Easter Island

Before You Read

A Check the statements that are true about you.

☐ 1. I enjoy seeing new places and doing new activities.
☐ 2. When I travel, I prefer to visit famous places that many people know about.
☐ 3. It is much better to travel to places that are easy to reach by plane or car.

B Look at the vocabulary and check the ones you know.

☐ native   ☐ isolated   ☐ region
☐ inhabitant   ☐ determine   ☐ descendant

Unit 13 57

Getting Away from It All

▸ *As you read, pay attention to what makes each place difficult to reach.*

Thanks to the Internet and international flights, the world is now a much smaller place. For instance, people can travel from South Korea to Argentina in almost one day. Nevertheless, a few places are still **isolated** from the rest of society.

Perhaps the most famous isolated place is Easter Island, Chile. Also called Rapa Nui, the island is over 5,000 kilometers away from the mainland. Almost all of its 6,000 citizens are descendants of the original Polynesian **natives**. The island is well known for its 887 large stone heads, called *moai*. To visit Easter Island, take a five-hour flight from Santiago, Chile.

Tristan da Cunha is a small volcanic island located in the South Atlantic Ocean. It is more than 1,600 kilometers away from both South America and Africa. The island has no airport. So, people must take a seven-day boat trip to get there. Today, the island has about 300 **inhabitants**. Most of them work in the fishing industry.

▲ Yamdrok in Tibe

European researchers wanted to **determine** the most remote place on Earth. What was their conclusion? Yamdrok Tso, Tibetan Plateau. The area has a large lake and is a three-week trip to the nearest cities. Since there are no roads in the **region**, visitors must walk for 20 days to reach there.

Even in our modern world, there are still many places to go and get away from it all. Words 211

Vocabulary in Context
Write the words in bold next to their correct definitions.

1. _____ separate from other places
2. _____ a person or animal that lives somewhere
3. _____ a person who was born in a particular place
4. _____ a particular area or part of a state or country
5. _____ to decide something because of evidence or facts

Reading Comprehension

1 **What is this passage mainly about?**

   a. parts of the world that are still isolated from society

   b. reasons that the world today is a much smaller place

   c. the most popular places for people to take vacations

   d. the ways modern technology has made our lives more comfortable

2 **Which is NOT true about Easter Island?**

   a. Its other name is Rapa Nui.

   b. It is part of the nation of Chile.

   c. The island has hundreds of large stone heads.

   d. All its citizens are descendants of the Polynesian natives.

3 **How can people reach Tristan da Cunha?**

   _____

4 **Which is NOT mentioned about Tristan da Cunha?**

   a. how many people live there
   b. where the island is located
   c. what jobs most people have
   d. who the inhabitants are descended from

5 **What can you guess about Yamdrok Tso from the passage?**

   a. It is the largest lake in Tibet.
   b. European researchers live there.
   c. It is a popular tourist destination.
   d. None of the people there have cars.

Reading Skill   *Categorizing information means to arrange information or items into different groups.*

Fill in the chart with the words in the box.

Easter Island	• The island is 5,000 kilometers away from the mainland. • Visitors must take a ❶_____ flight from Santiago.
Tristan da Cunha	• It is in the ❷_____ Ocean 1,600 kilometers from any mainland. • It can only be reached by ❸_____.
Yamdrok Tso	• The region is considered the most ❹_____ place on Earth. • Visitors have to ❺_____ for 20 days to get there.

| boat | walk | five-hour | remote | South Atlantic |

Unit 13 59

Summary

Use the words and phrases in the box to complete the summary.

stone heads	weeklong	three weeks	isolated	airport

In spite of our advanced technology, many places remain ❶_____ from the rest of the world. One such place is Easter Island. This island is 5,000 kilometers away from Chile. It is most famous for its 887 large ❷_____ called *moai*. Another remote island is Tristan da Cunha. The island has no ❸_____ and can only be reached by a ❹_____ boat trip. The most remote place in the world is Yamdrok Tso in Tibet. It takes almost ❺_____ to get to the region since there are no roads.

Vocabulary Expansion

A Match the words with their similar meanings from the box.

remote	decide	citizen

Words	Similar Meaning
isolated	_____
inhabitant	_____
determine	_____

B Fill in the blanks using the words in bold from the passage. Change the forms if necessary.

1. Police still have not _____ the cause of the fire.
2. Some of the low areas in the _____ flood during the summer rains.
3. When we went hiking, we found an _____ cabin in the deep woods.
4. Tokyo is the largest city in the world with over 35,000,000 _____.
5. The tigers are a _____ of Asia. They originally came from Turkey to east Russia.

Theme | *Health*
Reading Skill | *Cause & Effect*

Unit 14

Sleep and Remember!

Before You Read

A Are you helping your brain work the best it can? Take this lifestyle quiz to find out.

1. Do you sleep at least 7 hours each night?
2. Do you ever stay up late doing homework or studying?
3. Do you ever have trouble memorizing new information?

B Look at the vocabulary and check the ones you know.

☐ enhance ☐ sort ☐ review
☐ stay up ☐ cram ☐ bother

Sleep and Remember!

▸ *As you read, pay attention to the ways sleep affects our brains.*

Many students **stay up** all night **cramming** for a big test the next day. However, new research suggests that getting a good night's sleep can greatly **enhance** our study performance.

While we sleep, we go through a stage called REM, or rapid eye movement, sleep. It helps us to remember things. During REM, the brain separates the information learned during the day. It works just like a bank teller sorting different types of money. Our brains remember and sort information such as vocabulary words, math problems, and ways to kick a soccer ball.

If people do not get REM sleep, they cannot remember as well. Studies have been done on two groups of people that have each studied the same list of vocabulary words. One group gets REM sleep, and the other does not. After sleeping, the people take a test on the words. The group that goes through REM sleep almost always does better on the test. The reason is the information is **reviewed** by their brains.

Also, sometimes the brain helps us make connections between different information during sleep. When we wake up, we suddenly realize the answer to a problem that was **bothering** us the night before. So, it turns out that the best way to solve your problems is to sleep on them.   Words 217

Vocabulary in Context
Write the words and phrases in bold next to their correct definitions.

1. _____ to give trouble to
2. _____ to improve or strengthen
3. _____ to remain awake; to not sleep
4. _____ to study or look at something again
5. _____ to memorize a lot of information in a short time

Reading Comprehension

1 What is the main idea of this passage?

a. REM means rapid eye movement sleep.
b. Sleeping before a test does not help.
c. Sleeping helps us to remember better.
d. Students who sleep a lot get the best grades.

2 Why did the people who got REM sleep do better on the test?

_____

3 Which is true according to the passage?

a. Cramming is the best way to prepare for a test.
b. Sleeping allows our brains to solve problems from the day before.
c. People who get REM sleep have a harder time remembering information.
d. It is uncommon for many students to stay up very late the night before a test.

4 What does NOT happen in the brain during the REM stage?

a. It becomes larger.   b. It sorts information.
c. It makes connections.   d. It reviews information.

5 According to the passage, what can you guess about many students' attitudes towards studying?

a. They think it is better to cram before a test.
b. They think it is better to review material every day.
c. They think it is better to take tests in the afternoon.
d. They think it is better to get a good night's sleep before a test.

Reading Skill *Cause and effect is when one event causes something to happen. The cause explains why something happens, and the effect is what happens as a result.*

Fill in the chart with the words in the box.

Cause	While we sleep, we go through the ❶_____ stage of sleep.
Effect	• It helps us to ❷_____ things and ❸_____ our study performance. • The brain ❹_____ the information we learned during the day. • The brain makes connections between ❺_____ information.

enhance	REM	different	separates	remember

Unit 14 63

Summary

Use the words in the box to complete the summary.

sorts	cramming	connections	realize	performance

❶_____ the night before a test is a bad idea. According to research, getting REM sleep can improve our study ❷_____. During REM sleep, rapid eye movement sleep, the brain is still working. The brain ❸_____ the information from the day, makes ❹_____ between information, and sometimes helps us to ❺_____ answers to annoying problems.

Vocabulary Expansion

A **Match the words with their similar meanings from the box.**

annoy	go over	arrange

Words	Similar Meaning
bother	_____
sort	_____
review	_____

B **Fill in the blanks using the words and phrases in bold from the passage. Change the forms if necessary.**

1. Could you please stop singing? It's really _____ me.

2. I had to _____ all night packing boxes for our move.

3. Even though I _____ all night for the test, I still got a bad grade.

4. You should _____ your essay to make sure there are no mistakes.

5. Studying hard and sleeping enough will _____ your school performance.

Theme | Technology
Reading Skill | Cause & Effect

Unit 15

Here Today, but Not for Much Longer

◀ Mail collection box

Before You Read

A Do you keep up with modern technology? Take this technology habits quiz to find out.

1. Do you listen to music on cassettes or CDs?
2. Do you use digital e-readers or other electronic books?
3. Do you ever send paper letters to others in the mail?

B Look at the vocabulary and check the ones you know.

☐ drop off ☐ portable ☐ import
☐ interactive ☐ efficient ☐ experiment

Here Today, but Not for Much Longer

▶ As you read, think about why new technologies are replacing older ones.

Do you ever listen to music on vinyl records, cassettes, or even CDs? Thanks to **portable** MP3 players, you probably do not. Just like vinyl records, many other types of technology will soon disappear forever.

Within the next 20 years, paper textbooks will be gone. They will be replaced with e-readers and other computer-based formats. Students will benefit from having **interactive** textbooks. For example, students will be able to do math problems and see the answers on their tablets. They will also be able to perform science **experiments** on them.

Your neighborhood mail collection box is also going to disappear. Most people today send emails and text messages instead of letters. As a result, the amount of letters sent in the mail has become much less. This is why public mailboxes will only remain in busy areas in the future. Soon, you will only be able to drop off a letter at shopping centers and subway and bus stations.

Thomas Edison's incandescent light bulb will soon stop shining. Many countries have banned the **import** of incandescent light bulbs even though some people still prefer using them. Instead, people should use fluorescent bulbs and LED lights. These types of lights are better for the environment. The reason is they are more energy **efficient**. These and other new technologies will save us time, money, and effort.   Words 224

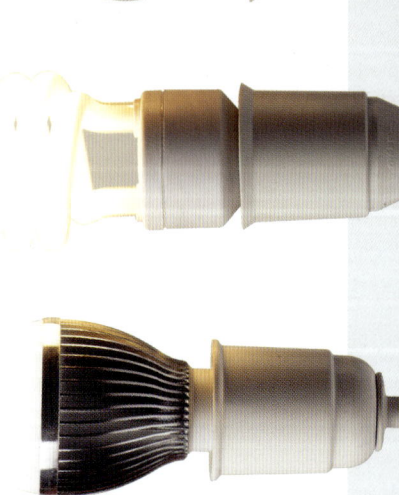

Vocabulary in Context
Write the words in bold next to their correct definitions.

1. _____ easy to carry or move around
2. _____ responding to the actions of a user
3. _____ working without wasting time, energy, or effort
4. _____ a scientific test done to see the effects of something
5. _____ the act of bringing a product into a country to be sold

Reading Comprehension

1 **What is the main idea of this passage?**

  a. New technologies are not always better than old ones.
  b. Most people want to send letters instead of using email.
  c. Old technologies are disappearing because of new developments.
  d. Listening to music on MP3 is better than listening to vinyl records.

2 **How will students benefit from electronic textbooks?**

  _____

3 **The main reason local mailboxes will be removed is** _____.

  a. they are too old and need to be replaced
  b. keeping them costs too much time and money
  c. the number of letters people mail has greatly decreased
  d. most people send their letters from shopping centers and subway stations

4 **Which is NOT true according to the passage?**

  a. Vinyl records have been replaced by newer technologies.
  b. Text messages and email are now more popular than letters.
  c. People can buy incandescent light bulbs anywhere in the world.
  d. E-readers will let students answer math problems in their books.

5 **You can guess that incandescent light bulbs** _____.

  a. were imported by Thomas Edison   b. are still sold in some countries
  c. use less energy than fluorescent lights   d. are not popular among consumers

Reading Skill
Cause and effect is when one event causes something to happen. The cause explains why something happens, and the effect is what happens as a result.

Fill in the chart with the words in the box.

Cause	Effect
• Digital textbooks will be more ❶_____.	• Traditional paper textbooks will be ❷_____.
• The amount of letters people send has ❸_____ very much.	• Most mailboxes will only remain in ❹_____ areas.
• Fluorescent and LED lights are more energy ❺_____.	• Many countries have banned the sale of incandescent light bulbs.

| replaced | efficient | interactive | fallen | crowded |

Unit 15 **67**

Summary

Use the words in the box to complete the summary.

| mailboxes | energy-efficient | letters | replacing | digital |

New technologies are always ❶_____ old ones. For instance, students in the future will no longer use paper textbooks. Instead, they will learn from interactive ❷_____ textbooks. Neighborhood ❸_____ are also disappearing. The reason is that most people today do not send ❹_____, but rather text messages and emails. Incandescent light bulbs are another technology that will soon be gone. More ❺_____ bulbs such as LEDs will take their place.

Vocabulary Expansion

A Some verbs can be followed by preposition. These two-word verbs are called phrased verbs. Match each phrase to a definition in the chart.

| drop off | drop in | drop out |

Words	Definition
_____	to quit school before finishing
_____	to leave something at a place and go
_____	to stop by and visit someone

B Fill in the blanks using the words in bold from the passage. Change the forms if necessary.

1. Computers use a keyboard and mouse because they are _____.
2. The first _____ televisions were actually heavy and hard to carry.
3. The government has allowed the _____ of rice from other countries.
4. They conducted an _____ to see the effect sleep has on creativity.
5. Our new air conditioners are up to 15 percent more _____ than the old models.

Theme | *Science*
Reading Skill | *Categorizing*

Unit 16

When One Baby Becomes Two

Before You Read

A How much do you know about twins? Check *T* or *F*.

1. Twins always look exactly alike.   T / F
2. Some twins have similar personalities and interests.   T / F
3. In some cases, twins are born with their bodies connected to each other.   T / F

B Look at the vocabulary and check the ones you know.

☐ fertilize   ☐ fraternal   ☐ divide
☐ behave   ☐ conjoined   ☐ identical

When One Baby Becomes Two

▶ *As you read, keep in mind how the different types of twins are created.*

Have you ever heard the terms "fraternal twins," "**identical** twins," or even "Siamese twins"? These are all different ways to describe the many different kinds of human twins.

The most common type of twins is fraternal twins. This happens when two of the mother's eggs are **fertilized** at the same time. This is unusual because women usually only make one egg at a time. Because they come from different eggs, the babies do not look exactly alike.

In the case of identical twins, only one egg is fertilized like a normal pregnancy. However, in very rare cases, the egg **divides** into two fertilized eggs. If this happens, twin babies will be born that look exactly alike. Studies show these two children will also **behave** in similar ways even if they are separated at birth.

The rarest type of twin is a "Siamese," or "**conjoined**," twin. A conjoined twin is when identical twins never actually separate. When they are born, their bodies may still be connected! One of the most famous pairs of conjoined twins was Chang and Eng Bunker. They were known as the first "Siamese Twins." They were born in Siam, now called Thailand. They became famous, and from them comes the expression "Siamese twins." **Words 206**

Vocabulary in Context
Write the words in bold next to their correct definitions.

1. _____ exactly alike
2. _____ to separate into parts
3. _____ to act in a certain way
4. _____ joined together; connected
5. _____ to make an egg able to grow and develop

Reading Comprehension

1 **What is this passage mainly about?**

a. why some twins look exactly alike
b. how a fertilized egg develops into a baby
c. the three types of twins and their characteristics
d. the reasons twins are more common these days

2 **Why do fraternal twins look different?**

_____

3 **Which is NOT true about fraternal twins?**

a. They look different from each other.
b. The egg divides into two fertilized eggs.
c. They are the most common kind of twins.
d. They come from two eggs fertilized at the same time.

4 **Which is true according to the passage?**

a. Siamese twins are born from the same egg.
b. Siamese twins are only born in one country.
c. There are more identical twins than the other types.
d. According to research, identical twins usually act differently.

5 **According to the passage, what can you guess about Siamese twins?**

a. Most of them are from Thailand.
b. They look identical to each other.
c. They behave similarly to fraternal twins.
d. We can see them often on the street.

Reading Skill _Categorizing information means to arrange information or items into different groups._

Fill in the chart with the words in the box.

	Types of Twins
Fraternal Twins	• happens when two eggs are ❶_____ at the same time • do not look ❷_____ alike
Identical Twins	• come from ❸_____ that divides • look exactly the same and often act ❹_____
Conjoined Twins	when identical twins never ❺_____

| one egg | fertilized | separate | similarly | exactly |

Unit 16 71

Summary

Use the words in the box to complete the summary.

fraternal	identical	rarest	divides	fertilized

Twins are classified into three types. The most common are ❶_____ twins. They are born when two separate eggs are ❷_____ at the same time. Another type is ❸_____ twins. They are born when one egg ❹_____ into two eggs. The ❺_____ type of twin is conjoined twins, which are born if a single egg never actually separates.

Vocabulary Expansion

A Match the words with their similar and opposite meanings from the box.

same	unusual	connect	different	separate	common

Words	Similar Meaning	Opposite Meaning
divide	_____	_____
identical	_____	_____
rare	_____	_____

B Fill in the blanks using the words in bold from the passage. Change the forms if necessary.

1. This river is actually two rivers that are _____.
2. Your picture looks _____ to the one I took yesterday.
3. I'm not sure how to _____ this pizza into five equal slices.
4. She looks like her brother, but she _____ very differently.
5. When a woman's egg becomes _____, she becomes pregnant.

Theme | *Astronomy*
Reading Skill | *Compare & Contrast*

Unit 17

Human vs. Robot Astronauts

Before You Read

A What do you know about space travel? Guess and circle the answers.

1. (Human / Robot) astronauts have been sent into Mars.
2. Only robots can be sent into space on (one-way / round-trip) missions.
3. The first person to walk on the moon was (Buzz Aldrin / Neil Armstrong).

B Look at the vocabulary and check the ones you know.

- ☐ advantage
- ☐ supplies
- ☐ fuel
- ☐ astronaut
- ☐ expense
- ☐ accomplishment

Summary

Use the words in the box to complete the summary.

astronauts   carry   advantages   accomplishment   expenses

Human astronauts need big and complicated spaceships to ❶_____ enough food, water, and air with them. This is why people are debating the ❷_____ of sending robots into space. The main benefit is there will be much fewer ❸_____. In addition, robot ❹_____ do not need to come back. On the other hand, people feel a sense of pride and ❺_____ with human astronauts' achievements. Neil Armstrong is a good example of this.

Vocabulary Expansion

A The suffix "-ment" means "condition" or "process." Add "-ment" to the words in the box and match each word to a definition in the chart.

develop	accomplish	manage

Words	Definition
_____	the act of controlling or dealing with something
_____	the act of causing something to grow or improve
_____	something done or achieved successfully

B Fill in the blanks using the words in bold from the passage. Change the forms if necessary.

1. Being able to play the piano is a major _____.

2. The main _____ of this laptop is its fast CPU.

3. My car ran out of _____ before we reached Miami.

4. Make a list of your _____ so we can repay you later.

5. When you go camping, you need to take enough _____.

Theme | *Art*
Reading Skill | *Sequencing*

Unit 18

Controversial Cave Paintings

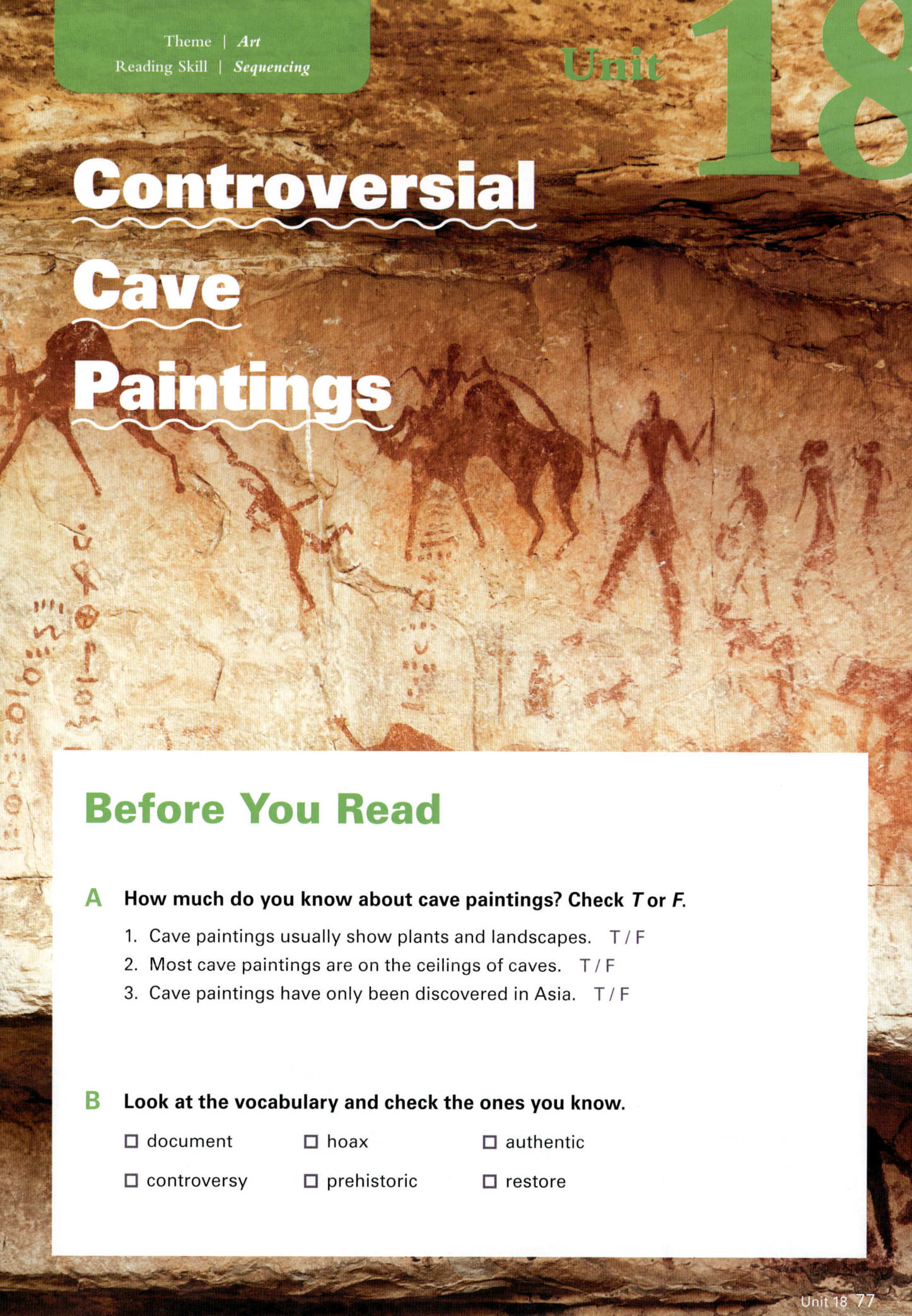

Before You Read

A How much do you know about cave paintings? Check *T* or *F*.

1. Cave paintings usually show plants and landscapes.   T / F
2. Most cave paintings are on the ceilings of caves.   T / F
3. Cave paintings have only been discovered in Asia.   T / F

B Look at the vocabulary and check the ones you know.

☐ document   ☐ hoax   ☐ authentic
☐ controversy   ☐ prehistoric   ☐ restore

Controversial Cave Paintings

▶ *As you read, pay attention to how people's opinions about the cave paintings changed.*

Interviewer	Maria Sautuola, tell us about the prehistoric cave paintings in the Altamira cave.
Maria	As you know, the cave is on my father's land in northern Spain. My father, Marcelino Sautuola, started exploring it in 1875. One day, he took me with him in 1879. I was the one who first noticed the shapes above us. I said, "Papa, look at the animals on the ceiling!" At once, he knew the paintings were prehistoric.
Interviewer	What were the paintings of?
Maria	There are a herd of bison, two horses, and a large deer on the ceiling.
Interviewer	What about the **controversy**?
Maria	My father invited a professor from the University of Madrid to help him **document** the paintings. The professor said they are about 16,000 years old. The public was very excited to read about them. But French archaeologists refused to believe the paintings were **authentic**. They said cavemen could not have made such paintings. My father was even accused of hiring a local artist to make a **hoax**. When he and the professor presented their work at a scientific convention in Lisbon in 1880, everyone laughed at them. It was an outrage!
Interviewer	Marcelino Sautuola died in 1888. In 1902, after some other cave paintings were found in Europe, the scientific community accepted the Altamira cave paintings as authentic. Fourteen years after he died, Sautuola's honor was **restored**. Words 223

Vocabulary in Context

Write the words in bold next to their correct definitions.

1. _____ not copied; real or true
2. _____ an issue that has many people for and against it
3. _____ a trick or lie that many people believe is true
4. _____ to return someone or something to an earlier good condition
5. _____ to make a record of something through writing or photography

Reading Comprehension

1 What is the main idea of this passage?

   a. Most new scientific discoveries are not true.
   b. Hoaxes are a big problem for many scientists.
   c. Cave paintings teach us what life was like in ancient times.
   d. The Altamira cave paintings were first considered a hoax.

2 Who first found the Altamira cave paintings?

   _____

3 Which is NOT true according to the passage?

   a. The paintings show a herd of bison, horses, and deer.
   b. The Altamira cave paintings are on the ceiling of the cave.
   c. Sautuola's honor was restored fourteen years after he died.
   d. A French archeologist helped Sautuola document the paintings.

4 Scientists said the paintings were too _____ for cavemen.

   a. simple   b. colorful   c. advanced   d. natural

5 According to the passage, you can guess that _____.

   a. the Altamira cave paintings were some of first to be found in Europe
   b. Sautuola was trying to attract tourists to his land by creating a hoax
   c. most scientists were excited about the discovery of the paintings in Altamira
   d. the professor from Madrid was paid by Sautuola to say the paintings were authentic

Reading Skill *Sequencing is putting events in order from first to last. When we sequence, we can easily understand which events happen first, second, and so on.*

Fill in the chart and number the events in order.

French archaeologists accused Sautuola of making a ❶_____.
Maria and her father Sautuola explored the ❷_____ and discovered ❸_____.
Other cave paintings were found, and Sautuola's honor was ❹_____.
A ❺_____ helped Sautuola document the paintings.

| Altamira cave | professor | hoax | restored | cave paintings |

Unit 18

Summary

Use the words in the box to complete the summary.

document	authentic	critical	daughter	hoax

The scientific community is sometimes very ❶_____ of new discoveries. This was the case for the Altamira cave paintings, discovered by Marcelino Sautuola's ❷_____ in 1879. Sautuola invited a professor from Madrid to help him ❸_____ the cave paintings. However, most other scientists thought the paintings were a ❹_____. Scientists finally accepted that the Altamira cave paintings were ❺_____ after many other cave paintings were found in Europe. Unfortunately, Sautuola had died by that time.

Vocabulary Expansion

A Match the words with their similar and opposite meanings from the box.

real	insult	pleasure	dispute	fake	agreement

Words	Similar Meaning	Opposite Meaning
outrage	_____	_____
authentic	_____	_____
controversy	_____	_____

B Fill in the blanks using the words in bold from the passage. Change the forms if necessary.

1. She was the victim of a mean _____.
2. Please take pictures to _____ my work.
3. We need to make sure that the signature is _____.
4. The workers are trying to _____ the house to its original condition.
5. The decision to get rid of Saturday classes created a lot of _____ among parents.

Theme | *Food*
Reading Skill | *Fact & Opinion*

Unit 19

Is Chocolate Good for You?

Before You Read

A How much do you know about chocolate? Check *T* or *F*.

1. All chocolate has high levels of sugar.   T / F
2. Chocolate can actually be healthy for you.   T / F
3. Dark chocolate has a greater percentage of cacao.   T / F

B Look at the vocabulary and check the ones you know.

- ☐ conclusive
- ☐ hype
- ☐ bitter
- ☐ consume
- ☐ run
- ☐ cardiovascular

Is Chocolate Good for You?

▶ *As you read, pay attention to the benefits and problems of eating chocolate.*

For years, most people considered chocolate just another candy, something that is tasty but unhealthy. Today, that is no longer the case. Many believe that eating chocolate can help you stay healthier. Is the idea that chocolate is healthy simply hype or is there some truth to these claims?

More and more evidence suggests that chocolate is healthy. One Harvard scientist studied the natives on a small island near Panama. He noticed they had very healthy **cardiovascular** systems. However, their relatives who left the island had less healthy cardiovascular systems. The reason was that the island natives drank three to four cups of cacao a day. Also, Dutch scientists studied older men who **consumed** a lot of cacao. They were less likely to die from any diseases. Moreover, a medical journal **ran** an article about people who regularly ate small amounts of dark chocolate. They have a lower risk of getting heart disease.

However, there are still many critics. Some scientists say that none of these studies are really **conclusive**. None of the studies were long term or were done with strict scientific controls. You should also remember that sweet chocolate bars might contain sugar and fattening calories. Be sure to check the labels carefully. Dark chocolate has a higher percentage of cacao. It is supposed to be better for you. But beware. A high percentage of cacao means a **bitter** taste.

Words 231

Vocabulary in Context

Write the words in bold next to their correct definitions.

1. _____ not sweet
2. _____ to eat or drink
3. _____ to print or broadcast a news story
4. _____ related to the heart and blood vessels
5. _____ containing enough evidence to prove something

Reading Comprehension

1 What is the main idea of this passage?

   a. Chocolate has been proven to make people fat.
   b. Chocolate may actually have some health benefits.
   c. Dark chocolate affects the cardiovascular system.
   d. Studies about the benefits of chocolate are not conclusive.

2 Who has a lower risk of getting heart disease?

   _____

3 Which is true according to the passage?

   a. Dark chocolate can be good for your health.
   b. Most of the studies were done over a long period.
   c. Only older men can benefit from eating dark chocolate.
   d. Studies have shown cacao can prevent some types of cancer.

4 How can consuming chocolate be unhealthy for you?

   a. Eating too much chocolate can weaken your heart.
   b. The bitter taste of dark chocolate can make you sick.
   c. Some types of chocolate have a lot of sugar and calories.
   d. Drinking cacao increases your chance of cardiovascular disease.

5 What can you guess about the island natives who left the island?

   a. They have lower rates of heart disease.
   b. They do not drink many cups of cacao daily.
   c. They will become the subjects of further medical tests.
   d. They became unhealthy because they ate two much fast food.

Reading Skill *A fact is a true statement that can be proven by evidence. An opinion is somebody's feelings about a subject. It may or may not be true.*

Write *F* for facts or *O* for opinions.

Statements	F or O
1. Drinking cacao can make your cardiovascular system healthier.	
2. There are not enough studies about the benefits of chocolate.	
3. Sweet chocolate bars taste better than dark chocolate bars.	
4. Dark chocolate can help lower the risk of getting heart disease.	

Summary

Use the words in the box to complete the summary.

cacao	image	long term	health	controls

Recently, the public ❶_____ of chocolate as a fattening, sweet candy has changed. Scientific studies suggest that dark chocolate might be a type of health food. Most of these studies indicate that eating ❷_____, which dark chocolate has a lot of, will help improve one's cardiovascular system. However, critics have pointed out that none of these studies were done over the ❸_____. Also, they were not carried out under strict scientific ❹_____. Finally, remember that only dark chocolate has these supposed ❺_____ benefits.

Vocabulary Expansion

A Match the words with their similar meanings from the box.

eat	decisive	usually

Words	Similar Meaning
conclusive	_____
regularly	_____
consume	_____

B Fill in the blanks using the words in bold from the passage. Change the forms if necessary.

1. There is a lot of evidence, but none of it is _____.
2. I don't drink coffee because I don't like its _____ taste.
3. The news _____ a story last night on how to eat healthier.
4. Driving your car fast _____ more fuel than driving it slowly does.
5. The best way to develop a healthy _____ system is to get lots of exercise.

Theme | *Education*
Reading Skill | *Cause & Effect*

Unit 20

What Was the Most Important Invention?

Before You Read

A   Check the statements that you agree with.

☐ 1. The Internet has made the world a better place.
☐ 2. Being able to write is not that important.
☐ 3. Humans must learn from past generations to make life better.

B   Look at the vocabulary and check the ones you know.

☐ invention   ☐ scholar   ☐ carve
☐ concept   ☐ generation   ☐ lecture

What Was the Most Important Invention?

▶ *As you read, think about how writing helps us to pass knowledge to future generations.*

Nobody really agrees on what the most important invention is. Some will say it was the wheel, and others will say computers. However, a very good choice would be writing. Without writing, knowledge and ideas would quickly become lost.

Once humans started to write, they could give their knowledge to future **generations**. Humans could **carve** stone, scratch on clay, and put ink on paper to draw symbols and letters. Because of writing, we can know more about the early Chinese or ancient Egyptians. More importantly, we can learn more quickly. We can read about the ideas that great minds before us took years to discover. Studying may seem to take a long time. However, it is faster than trying to figure things out by yourself. For example, there is no need to reinvent algebra. We can just read the book written by the inventor of algebra, Al-Khwarizmi, the Muslim mathematician.

Writing is important because humans do not live very long. Wise **scholars** cannot pass all their knowledge to future generations just by **lecturing**. Students cannot remember and repeat everything exactly. So, scholars write down what they know. That way, future students can study their **concepts** again and again. Then they can use this knowledge to make many new, wonderful inventions.   **Words 210**

Vocabulary in Context
Write the words in bold next to their correct definitions.

1. _____ a general idea about something
2. _____ an expert in a field of knowledge
3. _____ all the people in a certain age group
4. _____ to talk to students to teach them a certain subject
5. _____ to cut away at a hard surface to make a certain shape

Reading Comprehension

1 **What is the main idea of this passage?**

  a. Nobody can agree on what the most important invention is.
  b. The early Chinese and Egyptians both invented writing systems.
  c. Ancient scholars had to keep reinventing knowledge that was lost.
  d. Writing is the most important invention because it passes on knowledge.

2 **Which was NOT a method of writing mentioned in the passage?**

  a. carving stone
  b. burning into wood
  c. putting ink on paper
  d. scratching on clay

3 **How does writing help us to learn more quickly?**

  It helps us to read about _____ before us.

4 **Which is true according to the passage?**

  a. The Chinese invented algebra.
  b. Ancient people could only use paper to write.
  c. Studying is easier than coming up with new ideas.
  d. The best way to pass knowledge along is by lecturing.

5 **What would happen to a culture that died out and did not know about writing?**

  a. Scientists would research that culture very much.
  b. Today, we would not know much about that culture.
  c. People would want to learn more about that culture.
  d. There would be more of a need to bring back that culture.

Reading Skill   *Cause and effect is when one event causes something to happen. The cause explains why something happens, and the effect is what happens as a result.*

Fill in the chart with the words in the box.

Cause	Human beings began to use ❶_____.
Effect	• We can learn more about ❷_____ cultures. • We can study the ideas that great minds before us took years to ❸_____. • We can use the knowledge of past ❹_____ to make new inventions.

| discover | writing | ancient | generations |

Unit 20 87

Summary

Use the words in the box to complete the summary.

generations	ancestors	write	inventions	important

Writing is probably the most ❶_____ invention. In ancient times, humans drew symbols and letters to ❷_____ by carving stone, scratching on clay, and putting ink on paper. Without writing, knowledge of all other inventions could not be passed down accurately to future ❸_____. Because of writing, students do not have to reinvent basic concepts. They can quickly use the knowledge of their ❹_____ to make new and better ❺_____.

Vocabulary Expansion

A Match the words with their similar meanings from the box.

idea	talk	discovery

Words	Similar Meaning
invention	_____
concept	_____
lecture	_____

B Fill in the blanks using the words in bold from the passage. Change the forms if necessary.

1. The new _____ needs to learn about the past.
2. Today, our teacher _____ about different types of poems.
3. After many years of studying, he became a great _____ in his field.
4. The Romans _____ numbers and letters into stones in their buildings.
5. Students who want to study science in college should already know many basic _____.

Developing Background Knowledge and Reading Strategies

Reading
Voyage
2

BASIC

WORKBOOK

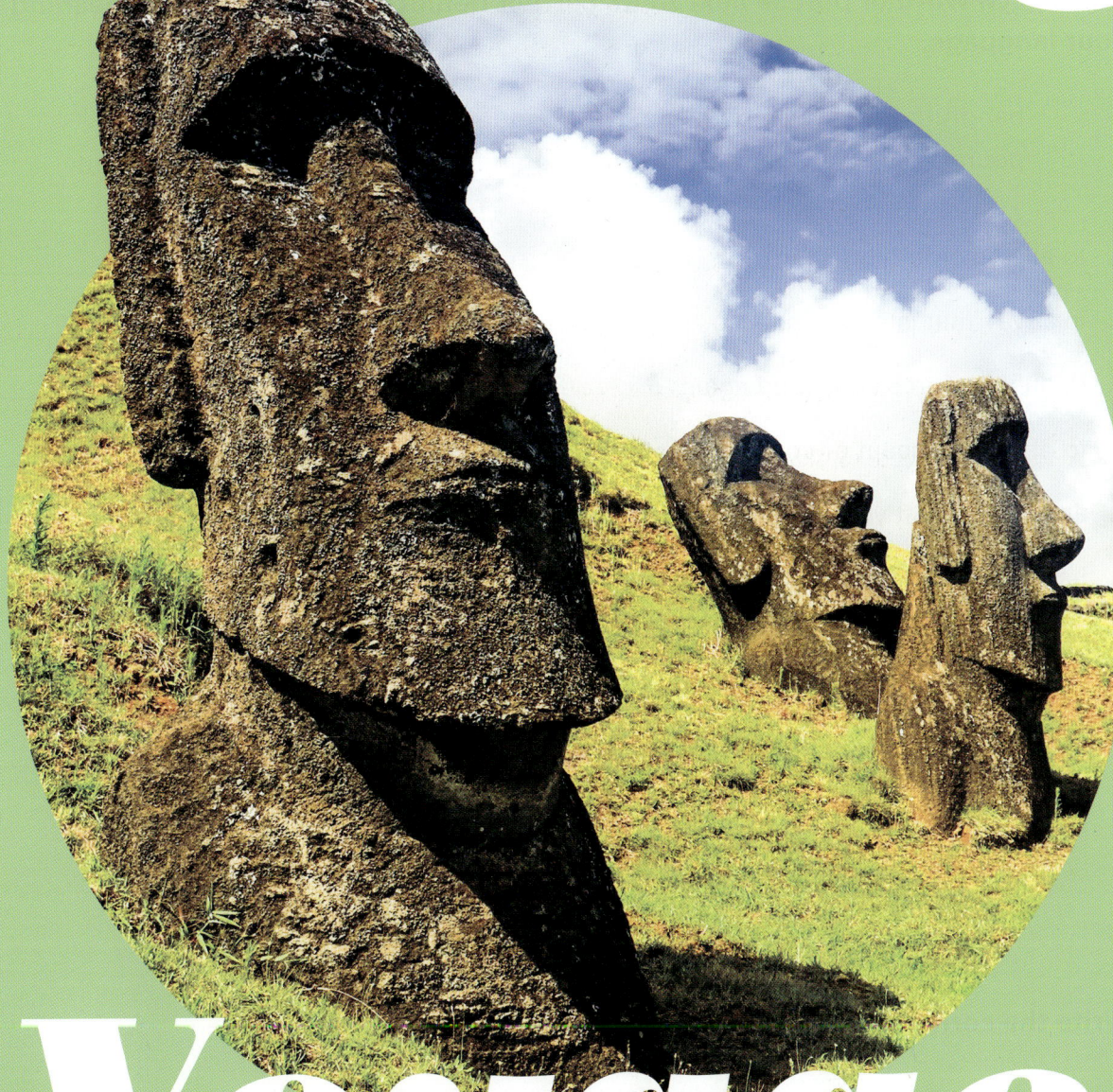

Unit 1 Beautiful Trash

Vocabulary Practice

A Write each word or phrase next to its correct definition. Then write its meaning in your language.

| handful | smooth | biodegradable | appliance |
| pound | permit | go through with | by accident |

1. to allow something　　　　　　　　　　_____　_____

2. in a way that is not planned　　　　　　_____　_____

3. to hit with force again and again　　　　_____　_____

4. to officially accept or complete a plan　_____　_____

5. an amount that you can hold in your hand　_____　_____

6. having a flat, even surface; not having bumps　_____　_____

7. capable of being broken down by natural processes　_____　_____

8. a machine that you have in your home such as a refrigerator　_____　_____

B Write the correct words to complete the sentences.

| dumped | allowed | ban | rough |

1. Smoking is not _____ in this restaurant.

2. Many factories have _____ toxic waste into the river.

3. One of the biggest snowstorms caused some _____ road conditions.

4. The city is going to _____ the consumption of alcohol in the park.

2

Writing Practice

A Unscramble the words to complete the sentences.

1. (have / seen / you / ever / a beach)

   ➤ _____ covered in pieces of glass?

2. (not / has / these / gone through / with / plans)

   ➤ The government _____.

3. (home / handfuls of / take / the / glass beads / smooth)

   ➤ Many visitors _____.

4. (was / accident / Glass Beach / created / by)

   ➤ _____.

5. (people / to / were / throw away / permitted / garbage / their)

   ➤ _____ in the ocean near the city.

B Translate the sentences into your language, focusing on the meanings of the underlined parts.

1. Glass Beach shows <u>how</u> nature can make our trash beautiful <u>over time</u>.

   ➤ _____

2. The glass was <u>too</u> difficult <u>to</u> remove, so it <u>was left</u> in the water.

   ➤ _____

3. The local government made <u>it</u> illegal <u>to throw away trash</u> in the water.

   ➤ _____

Unit 2 What Is a Geek?

Vocabulary Practice

A Write each word or phrase next to its correct definition. Then write its meaning in your language.

| horror | consider | stereotype | matter |
| passionate | in general | get along with | social skills |

1. to think of as _____ _____

2. to be important _____ _____

3. having strong feelings _____ _____

4. most of the time; usually _____ _____

5. the ability to get along well with others _____ _____

6. a painful feeling caused by great shock or fear _____ _____

7. to have a friendly relationship with someone _____ _____

8. an unfair or untrue belief about a specific group of people _____ _____

B Write the correct words to complete the sentences.

| matter | believed | typically | enthusiastic |

1. The courses _____ last for six months.

2. It is _____ that the house was built in 1657.

3. For a while, Sarah was _____ about taking piano lessons.

4. It doesn't _____ if you lock the door or not. This neighborhood is very safe.

4

Writing Practice

A Unscramble the words to complete the sentences.

1. (hard / them / friends / for / it / to / make)
   ▶ This stereotype makes _____.

2. (asked / what / was / me / a geek / you)
   ▶ In your last letter, _____.

3. (most people / how / about / computers / more than / work)
   ▶ They know _____.

4. (who / really / anything / are / people / about / passionate)
   ▶ Actually, geeks can be _____.

5. (someone / a / playing / if / likes / game / certain)
   ▶ _____, that person can be called a geek.

B Translate the sentences into your language, focusing on the meanings of the underlined parts.

1. It doesn't matter <u>if</u> it's a computer game <u>or not</u>.
   ▶ _____

2. Other students <u>considered</u> my friends and me <u>to be</u> geeks.
   ▶ _____

3. Geeks <u>are</u> usually <u>defined as</u> people who <u>are</u> really <u>interested in</u> new technology.
   ▶ _____

Unit 3: Cheering for Cheerleaders

Vocabulary Practice

A Write each word or phrase next to its correct definition. Then write its meaning in your language.

whip up	stunt	appreciate	beat
out of shape	squad	responsibility	row

1. in poor physical condition _____ _____
2. a physical action showing skill _____ _____
3. a straight line of people or things _____ _____
4. to defeat someone in a competition _____ _____
5. something that is your job or duty to do _____ _____
6. to admire or value someone or something _____ _____
7. a small group of people who work together _____ _____
8. to cause people to have strong feelings about something _____ _____

B Write the correct words to complete the sentences.

responsibility	acceptability	appreciate	possibility

1. There is a _____ that it will snow today.
2. Love is a form of _____ and duty to family.
3. The project suffered from a lack of social _____.
4. Mr. Jackson teaches students how to _____ good movies.

Writing Practice

A **Unscramble the words to complete the sentences.**

1. (called / football / is / team / the Titans)
   ➤ Their _____.

2. (to / Matt's / is / responsibilities / chants / invent)
   ➤ One of _____.

3. (itself / become / cheerleading / has / a sport)
   ➤ These days, _____.

4. (climb up / make / third / a / to / row / cheerleaders)
   ➤ Then two more _____.

5. (strongest / line up / the other / side-by-side / cheerleaders)
   ➤ Matt and three of _____.

B **Translate the sentences into your language, focusing on the meanings of the underlined parts.**

1. Matt's squad does <u>not just</u> brainstorm <u>chants to yell</u> at games.
   ➤ _____

2. They <u>help</u> three other cheerleaders <u>climb up</u> to stand on their shoulders.
   ➤ _____

3. Many male students also help <u>whip up</u> support for their school's team.
   ➤ _____

Unit 3 7

Unit 4 Solved Mysteries

Vocabulary Practice

A Write each word next to its correct definition. Then write its meaning in your language.

| solve | track | mystery | sink |
| slippery | baffle | observation | cursed |

1. to confuse someone completely   _____   _____

2. to find an answer to a problem   _____   _____

3. to go down below the surface of water   _____   _____

4. the act of careful watching or listening _____   _____

5. something strange that cannot be explained or understood   _____   _____

6. a mark left in the ground by a moving person, animal, or vehicle   _____   _____

7. affected by a mysterious power that causes bad things to happen   _____   _____

8. difficult to stand or move on because of being smooth, wet, or icy   _____   _____

B Write the correct words to complete the sentences.

| observation | solvable | observable | solution |

1. I think all problems are _____.

2. The data were collected by careful _____.

3. That's not a good _____ to this problem.

4. There is no _____ difference between these events.

Writing Practice

A Unscramble the words to complete the sentences.

1. (the / leaves / ground / slippery)
    ▶ The flooding _____.

2. (is / the / believe / cursed / that / area)
    ▶ Some people _____.

3. (have / "sailing stones" / people / for / baffled / decades)
    ▶ The so-called _____.

4. (using / can / explained / science and observation / be)
    ▶ Almost all of them _____.

5. (already / have / been / many of / solved / these mysteries)
    ▶ It turns out that _____.

B Translate the sentences into your language, focusing on the meanings of the underlined parts.

1. The area where the stones are sometimes floods.
    ▶ _____

2. This makes it seem like the stones move due to a mysterious power.
    ▶ _____

3. The percentage of ships that sink in the Bermuda Triangle is about the same as in the rest of the ocean.
    ▶ _____

Unit 4 9

Unit 5 — Technology Rivals

Vocabulary Practice

A Write each word or phrase next to its correct definition. Then write its meaning in your language.

| found | interface | revolutionize | drop out |
| competitor | step down | operating system | release |

1. to start an organization or a company _____ _____

2. to make something available to the public _____ _____

3. to leave school without finishing your studies _____ _____

4. to leave a job or official position; to resign _____ _____

5. to change something very much or completely _____ _____

6. a system that a person uses to control a computer _____ _____

7. a set of programs that control the way a computer system works _____ _____

8. someone who is trying to win or do better than others in sports or business _____ _____

B Write the correct words or phrases to complete the sentences.

| created | resign | operating system | rivals |

1. She _____ the company to realize her dream.

2. The two companies have been _____ for a long time.

3. Upgrade the _____, and your tablet becomes a new device.

4. The main reason behind his decision to _____ is the fact that his salary is too low.

10

Writing Practice

A **Unscramble the words to complete the sentences.**

1. (leave / in / forced / Apple / was / to / 1985)
   ➤ Jobs _____.

2. (much / had / in / but / common / the two men)
   ➤ They were serious competitors, _____.

3. (on / developing / software / MS-DOS / focused / such as)
   ➤ From the beginning, Gates _____.

4. (of / manage / to / certain parts / continues / the company)
   ➤ However, he _____.

5. (college / their / left / to / own / found / computer companies / early)
   ➤ Both of them _____.

B **Translate the sentences into your language, focusing on the meanings of the underlined parts.**

1. Bill Gates stepped down as CEO of Microsoft in 2000.
   ➤ _____

2. Apple was the first company to make the computer mouse popular.
   ➤ _____

3. Both were highly successful, creating products that millions of people use today.
   ➤ _____

Unit 5   11

Unit 6 Who Discovered America First?

Vocabulary Practice

A Write each word or phrase next to its correct definition. Then write its meaning in your language.

| explorer | spread | evidence | introduce |
| all the way | discover | out loud | in addition |

1. to distribute   _____   _____
2. as something more   _____   _____
3. a clue or sign of something _____   _____
4. going completely or fully   _____   _____
5. to find a place for the first time _____   _____
6. say something so others can hear   _____   _____
7. to show something new to others   _____   _____
8. a person who travels to places to find something _____   _____

B Write the correct words to complete the sentences.

| recall | keep | find | stop |

1. The traffic light turned red, so she had to _____.
2. I'm always happy to _____ some money in my coat pockets.
3. I wanted to call her, but I couldn't _____ her phone number.
4. I _____ on telling you not to send money to him, but you won't listen.

Writing Practice

A **Unscramble the words to complete the sentences.**

1. (what / now / is / to the east coast of / Canada)
   ▶ They made it _____.

2. (introduced / that / the Americas / say / Columbus / to Europe)
   ▶ We can _____.

3. (along / Viking camps / some evidence / of / the Canadian coast)
   ▶ There is still _____.

4. (Columbus / the first person / not / to discover America / was / see that)
   ▶ We can _____.

5. (America / this sentence / Columbus / to remember / use / when / discovered)
   ▶ Many students _____.

B **Translate the sentences into your language, focusing on the meanings of the underlined parts.**

1. He was the first <u>to spread</u> this news to all Europeans.
   ▶ _____

2. They went <u>all the way</u> down <u>through</u> Central America <u>into</u> South America.
   ▶ _____

3. They crossed an ice bridge <u>from</u> eastern Russia <u>to</u> Alaska thousands of years ago.
   ▶ _____

The Haka, a Maori Tradition

Vocabulary Practice

A Write each word or phrase next to its correct definition. Then write its meaning in your language.

| slap | achievement | warrior | stamp |
| enemy | discourage | poke out | individually |

1. a soldier, especially in the past _____ _____
2. separately and not as a group _____ _____
3. something that results from hard work _____ _____
4. a group of people you fight against in a war _____ _____
5. to make someone less hopeful or confident _____ _____
6. to put your foot down heavily and noisily on the ground _____ _____
7. to hit something with the front or back of your hand _____ _____
8. to stick out something so that part of it can be seen _____ _____

B Write the correct words to complete the sentences.

| requirements | achievements | discouragement | discouraging |

1. Our teachers are very proud of all of our _____.
2. My brother has fulfilled the _____ for graduation.
3. The negative feedback has been _____ the actors.
4. When you lose confidence, _____ is just around the corner.

14

Writing Practice

A **Unscramble the words to complete the sentences.**

1. (by / performed / group / a / is)
   ▶ The haka _____.

2. (forms / the haka / of / different / exist)
   ▶ Many _____.

3. (to / used / celebrate / was / achievements / special)
   ▶ The haka _____.

4. (for / cultural / the Maori / important / an / tradition / people)
   ▶ The haka is _____.

5. (remain / will / for many years / popular / to come / the haka)
   ▶ _____.

B **Translate the sentences into your language, focusing on the meanings of the underlined parts.**

1. They think it was a war dance to frighten enemies.
   ▶ _____

2. *Peruperu* was performed before a battle to discourage the enemy.
   ▶ _____

3. Its purpose was to help the warriors prepare mentally for battle.
   ▶ _____

Unit 8 Subway Operators

Vocabulary Practice

A Write each word or phrase next to its correct definition. Then write its meaning in your language.

| candidate | operate | procedure | occur |
| emergency | be on the lookout | extensive | operator |

1. to happen _____ _____
2. covering a large area _____ _____
3. the usual way of doing something _____ _____
4. to cause to work or be in action _____ _____
5. a person who is being considered for a job _____ _____
6. an unexpected and dangerous situation _____ _____
7. to watch carefully for something to avoid danger, etc. _____ _____
8. someone whose job is to control a machine or vehicle _____ _____

B Write the correct words to complete the sentences.

| occur | control | process | extensive |

1. The pipe burst and caused _____ damage to his house.
2. The programmer can _____ the robot's movement.
3. Terrorists attacks can _____ anywhere in the world.
4. Studying to become a lawyer is a long _____ over many years.

16

Writing Practice

A Unscramble the words to complete the sentences.

1. (are / subway operators / most / controlled / trains / by)
   ▶ The fact is that _____.

2. (operate / how / different / trains / types / to / of)
   ▶ Applicants learn _____.

3. (must / written / candidates / exams / pass)
   ▶ After the training is done, _____.

4. (an operator / driving / of / the trains / is / responsibility)
   ▶ The main _____.

5. (make sure / is / attention / everyone / to / safe / pay)
   ▶ Operators must always _____.

B Translate the sentences into your language, focusing on the meanings of the underlined parts.

1. Being a subway operator can be an exciting job.
   ▶ _____

2. Candidates who fail these exams cannot become operators.
   ▶ _____

3. They learn what to do when there is a stopped train ahead.
   ▶ _____

Unit 9 — Theories about the Earth

Vocabulary Practice

A Write each word next to its correct definition. Then write its meaning in your language.

| continent | solid | theory | float |
| observe | disprove | complex | geologist |

1. difficult to understand _____ _____
2. a very large land mass _____ _____
3. having no space inside; firm or hard _____ _____
4. a scientist who studies the Earth _____ _____
5. to show that something is wrong or false _____ _____
6. a system of ideas that explains something _____ _____
7. to stay on the surface of a liquid and not go under _____ _____
8. to watch something carefully to get information about it _____ _____

B Write the correct words to complete the sentences.

| disconnected | disappeared | floated | disprove |

1. The moon _____ behind the clouds.
2. The little paper boat _____ on the water.
3. It took several months to _____ their claim.
4. We were talking on the phone when suddenly we got _____.

Writing Practice

A **Unscramble the words to complete the sentences.**

1. (about / what / all / is / science)
   ➤ That is _____.

2. (completely / with / may / new / change / discoveries)
   ➤ Our ideas about the Earth today _____.

3. (melted / hot / that / the Earth / rocks / was / so)
   ➤ He said the inside of _____.

4. (this / named / true / not / was / said / Alfred Wegener)
   ➤ In 1912, a geologist _____.

5. (moving / for millions of years / have / slowly / the continents / been)
   ➤ He thought _____.

B **Translate the sentences into your language, focusing on the meanings of the underlined parts.**

1. We should change our ideas <u>to fit</u> the new evidence.
   ➤ _____

2. The Earth is <u>so</u> complex <u>that</u> it will take a long time <u>to learn</u> all of its secrets.
   ➤ _____

3. Most scientists <u>laughed at</u> his ideas, but later observations <u>proved that</u> he was right.
   ➤ _____

Unit 10 Western Individuals, Eastern Groups

Vocabulary Practice

A Write each word or phrase next to its correct definition. Then write its meaning in your language.

pity	express	globalized	coworker
conform	approach	highlight	get away

1. a person who you work with _____ _____

2. to mark or emphasize something _____ _____

3. involving or affecting the entire world _____ _____

4. a feeling of sorrow for someone else _____ _____

5. to communicate by words or behavior _____ _____

6. a way of considering or doing something _____ _____

7. to change oneself to be similar to society _____ _____

8. to leave or escape from a person or place _____ _____

B Write the correct words to complete the sentences.

obey	show	emphasize	approach

1. Let me _____ you a chart to help you understand.

2. Drivers need to _____ traffic signals and signs.

3. He proposed a new _____ to helping the homeless.

4. We can _____ our main points by using our hands.

Writing Practice

A Unscramble the words to complete the sentences.

1. (unusual / things / do / it / to / alone / is)
   ➤ Many Asians think _____.

2. (need / to / own / their / more often / space)
   ➤ Westerners seem _____.

3. (if / alone / see / they / is eating / a person / who)
   ➤ _____, they may feel pity for that person.

4. (life / different / understand / these / cultural approaches / to)
   ➤ It is important to _____.

5. (make / conform / act / that person / to / and / like everyone else)
   ➤ Others will try _____.

B Translate the sentences into your language, focusing on the meanings of the underlined parts.

1. Neither style is basically good or bad.
   ➤ _____

2. Many westerners think it is strange to do everything as a group.
   ➤ _____

3. Many like to get away from their coworkers to have lunch with only a newspaper for company.
   ➤ _____

Unit 11 Lost in Time

Vocabulary Practice

A Write each word or phrase next to its correct definition. Then write its meaning in your language.

| curved | die out | examine | odd |
| muscular | deformed | alongside | ancient |

1. not normal _____ _____
2. not straight _____ _____
3. analyze; prove; study _____ _____
4. having large strong muscles _____ _____
5. from a very long time ago _____ _____
6. shaped in an unusual way _____ _____
7. to disappear completely _____ _____
8. at the same time as something else _____ _____

B Write the correct words or phrases to complete the sentences.

| examined | strange | rounded | together with |

1. Her handwriting was neat and _____.
2. Their meal arrived, _____ glasses of water.
3. The detectives _____ the crime scene, looking for clues.
4. The neighbors thought he was very _____ since he never wore shoes.

Writing Practice

A Unscramble the words to complete the sentences.

1. (I / thought / a / man / was / deformed)
   ▶ At first, scientists _____.

2. (by / discovered / in / were / miners / 1856)
   ▶ My bones _____.

3. (Charles Darwin's / book / on / famous / read / evolution)
   ▶ King had _____.

4. (they / into / my lands / came out of Africa, / moved)
   ▶ When *Homo sapiens* _____.

5. (were / where / found / because of / my bones / Neanderthal man)
   ▶ He called me _____.

B Translate the sentences into your language, focusing on the meanings of the underlined parts.

1. They were <u>thicker</u> and <u>more</u> curved <u>than</u> normal human bones.
   ▶ _____

2. We lived <u>alongside</u> them for thousands of years <u>until</u> the last of us died out.
   ▶ _____

3. The results show humans <u>like</u> me lived <u>between</u> 200,000 <u>and</u> 30,000 years ago.
   ▶ _____

Unit 12 Funny Product Names

Vocabulary Practice

A Write each word next to its correct definition. Then write its meaning in your language.

| grave | gross | sweat | mistranslate |
| disgust | ancestor | character | neighborhood |

1. very unpleasant _____ _____

2. a feeling of strong dislike _____ _____

3. a printed or written letter or symbol _____ _____

4. an area of a town or a city that people live in _____ _____

5. a place in the ground where a dead person is buried _____ _____

6. the liquid that is on your skin when you are hot _____ _____

7. a person in your family who lived a long time ago _____ _____

8. to change words from one language into another incorrectly _____ _____

B Write the correct words to complete the sentences.

| mislead | mistranslated | grave | misunderstand |

1. The translator _____ some of what I said.

2. She recently visited the _____ of her grandfather.

3. Don't _____ her. She's really a very nice person.

4. The president said that he didn't mean to _____ the public.

24

Writing Practice

A **Unscramble the words to complete the sentences.**

1. (trouble / foreign / have / in / countries)
    ▶ Even big companies _____.

2. (sounds / to / gross / many Americans / the name)
    ▶ I didn't realize it, but _____.

3. (that / means / "calzone" / in / "underwear" / Spanish)
    ▶ The restaurant didn't know _____.

4. (make / "ke-kou-ke-la" / the sound / to / Chinese characters)
    ▶ It was spelled with _____.

5. (the word / to / with / drink something / in the name / "sweat")
    ▶ They don't want _____.

B **Translate the sentences into your language, focusing on the meanings of the underlined parts.**

1. To them, it <u>sounds like</u> the can contains sweat from some guy <u>named</u> Pocari!
    ▶ _____

2. <u>When</u> I took it out of my lunchbox, my American friends looked at it <u>with disgust</u>.
    ▶ _____

3. You would <u>be surprised by how</u> some product names <u>are mistranslated</u> in different languages.
    ▶ _____

Getting Away from It All

Vocabulary Practice

A Write each word next to its correct definition. Then write its meaning in your language.

| region | isolated | inhabitant | volcanic |
| native | determine | descendant | remote |

1. produced by volcano   _____   _____
2. separate from other places   _____   _____
3. far away from any towns or cities   _____   _____
4. a person or animal that lives somewhere   _____   _____
5. a person who was born in a particular place   _____   _____
6. someone who lives after you, such as
   your child or grandchild   _____   _____
7. to decide something because of evidence
   or facts   _____   _____
8. a particular area or part of a state or country   _____   _____

B Write the correct words to complete the sentences.

| descendant | remote | citizen | decide |

1. I'll _____ what to do next after having dinner.
2. He can change his nationality to become a US _____.
3. It was revealed that she was the _____ of the last king.
4. The family lived in a _____ village without electricity.

Writing Practice

A **Unscramble the words to complete the sentences.**

1. (a seven-day / to / take / get / boat trip / there)
    ➤ People must _____.

2. (place / determine / the / remote / most / Earth / on)
    ➤ European researchers wanted to _____.

3. (are / a few / isolated / from / places / the rest of society)
    ➤ Nevertheless, _____.

4. (both / 1,600 kilometers / from / away / South America and Africa)
    ➤ The island is more than _____.

5. (get away from / many / still / are / places / to / there / it all)
    ➤ Even in our modern world, _____.

B **Translate the sentences into your language, focusing on the meanings of the underlined parts.**

1. The island is <u>well known for</u> its 887 large stone heads, <u>called</u> *moai*.
    ➤ _____

2. <u>Since</u> there are no roads in the region, visitors <u>must</u> walk for 20 days <u>to reach</u> there.
    ➤ _____

3. <u>Thanks to</u> the Internet and international flights, the world is now a <u>much smaller</u> place.
    ➤ _____

Unit 13 27

Unit 14 Sleep and Remember!

Vocabulary Practice

A Write each word or phrase next to its correct definition. Then write its meaning in your language.

| enhance | bother | review | sort |
| stay up | performance | turn out | cram |

1. to give trouble to _____ _____
2. how well you do something _____ _____
3. to improve or strengthen _____ _____
4. to have a particular result _____ _____
5. to study or look at something again _____ _____
6. to remain awake; to not sleep _____ _____
7. to memorize a lot of information in a short time _____ _____
8. to put things into different groups or types or into an order _____ _____

B Write the correct words or phrases to complete the sentences.

| go over | arranged | turned out | annoys |

1. We have _____ the files in alphabetical order.
2. Can you _____ this report and correct any mistakes?
3. It _____ that we graduated from the same high school.
4. It really _____ me when you don't listen to what I'm saying.

28

Writing Practice

A Unscramble the words to complete the sentences.

1. (always / does better / the / almost / test / on)
   ▶ The group that goes through REM sleep _____.

2. (reviewed / their brains / is / by / the information)
   ▶ The reason is _____.

3. (to solve / the best way / is / on / to sleep / them / your problems)
   ▶ It turns out that _____.

4. (all night / for / stay up / the next day / cramming / a big test)
   ▶ Many students _____.

5. (the information / during / the brain / the day / separates / learned)
   ▶ During REM, _____.

B Translate the sentences into your language, focusing on the meanings of the underlined parts.

1. The brain works just like a bank teller sorting different types of money.
   ▶ _____

2. Studies have been done on two groups of people that have each studied the same list of vocabulary words.
   ▶ _____

3. We suddenly realize the answer to a problem that was bothering us the night before.
   ▶ _____

Unit 15 Here Today, but Not for Much Longer

Vocabulary Practice

A Write each word or phrase next to its correct definition. Then write its meaning in your language.

| import | portable | drop off | ban |
| efficient | interactive | experiment | benefit |

1. to be helped _____ _____

2. easy to carry or move around _____ _____

3. responding to the actions of a user _____ _____

4. to say officially that something is not allowed _____ _____

5. to take something to a place and leave it there _____ _____

6. working without wasting time, energy, or effort _____ _____

7. a scientific test done to see the effects of something _____ _____

8. the act of bringing a product into a country to be sold _____ _____

B Write the correct words or phrases to complete the sentences.

| drop in | drop off | dropped out | banned |

1. He _____ of school in the eighth grade.

2. We went to our hotel to _____ our luggage.

3. The city has _____ swimming in the lake.

4. Please _____ anytime, we'll be happy to see you.

Writing Practice

A Unscramble the words to complete the sentences.

1. (are / energy / they / efficient / more)
    ▶ The reason is _____.

2. (having / benefit / textbooks / from / interactive)
    ▶ Students will _____.

3. (perform / to / science experiments / be / on / able / their tablets)
    ▶ Students will _____.

4. (only / in / why / public / remain / mailboxes / busy areas / will)
    ▶ This is _____.

5. (of / banned / light bulbs / have / the import / incandescent)
    ▶ Many countries _____.

B Translate the sentences into your language, focusing on the meanings of the underlined parts.

1. Within the next 20 years, paper textbooks will be gone.
    ▶ _____

2. As a result, the amount of letters sent in the mail has become much less.
    ▶ _____

3. Paper textbooks will be replaced with e-readers and other computer-based formats.
    ▶ _____

Unit 16 When One Baby Becomes Two

Vocabulary Practice

A Write each word next to its correct definition. Then write its meaning in your language.

identical	divide	term	fraternal
conjoined	fertilize	behave	common

1. exactly alike _____ _____
2. happening often _____ _____
3. to separate into parts _____ _____
4. to act in a certain way _____ _____
5. joined together; connected _____ _____
6. produced from different eggs _____ _____
7. a word or phrase that has an exact meaning _____ _____
8. to make an egg able to grow and develop _____ _____

B Write the correct words to complete the sentences.

unusual	separated	connected	common

1. The worker carefully _____ the two wires.
2. It's _____ for teenagers to sleep late at night.
3. It is _____ for Sue to be late. I hope she's okay.
4. This movie is _____ into several episodes for television.

Writing Practice

A **Unscramble the words to complete the sentences.**

1. (expression / the / comes / "Siamese Twins")
    ▶ From them _____.

2. (may / be / still / their / connected / bodies)
    ▶ When they are born, _____.

3. (twins / common / is / of / fraternal twins / most / type)
    ▶ The _____.

4. (women / only / one egg / make / because / at a time / usually)
    ▶ This is unusual _____.

5. (born / look / will / exactly / be / alike / twin babies / that)
    ▶ If this happens, _____.

B **Translate the sentences into your language, focusing on the meanings of the underlined parts.**

1. A conjoined twin is <u>when</u> identical twins <u>never</u> actually <u>separate</u>.
    ▶ _____

2. This happens <u>when</u> two of the mother's eggs are fertilized <u>at the same time</u>.
    ▶ _____

3. Studies show these two children will behave <u>in similar ways</u> <u>even if</u> they are separated at birth.
    ▶ _____

Human vs. Robot Astronauts

Vocabulary Practice

A Write each word next to its correct definition. Then write its meaning in your language.

| supplies | fuel | advantage | reveal |
| expense | astronaut | accomplishment | mission |

1. a benefit; a gain _____ _____

2. an energy source _____ _____

3. money paid for something _____ _____

4. to let something become known _____ _____

5. someone who travels and works in space _____ _____

6. the things such as fool, fuel, etc. that are needed by a group _____ _____

7. an important task, usually traveling somewhere _____ _____

8. something done or achieved successfully; an achievement _____ _____

B Write the correct words to complete the sentences.

| accomplishment | management | astronauts | development |

1. Children's books can benefit their _____.

2. The company offers financial _____ as a service.

3. Winning the award would be the most exciting _____ of his career.

4. Most _____ have dreamed of going to space since they were young.

Writing Practice

A **Unscramble the words to complete the sentences.**

1. (return / lucky / were / to / alive)
   ➤ The astronauts _____.

2. (enough / with / supplies / them / carry)
   ➤ Humans have to _____.

3. (humans / controlled / from / are / by / Earth)
   ➤ Today, robots on Mars _____.

4. (the moon / human astronauts / to / carried / three)
   ➤ The Apollo 13 spaceship _____.

5. (to / the moon / the first / set / human / foot / on)
   ➤ In 1969, Neil Armstrong was _____.

B **Translate the sentences into your language, focusing on the meanings of the underlined parts.**

1. On the way, one of the oxygen tanks <u>accidentally</u> exploded.
   ➤ _____

2. A smaller spaceship needs <u>less fuel</u> and has <u>fewer expenses</u>.
   ➤ _____

3. Both Russia and America <u>have been sending</u> robots to Mars <u>since</u> 1964.
   ➤ _____

Unit 18 Controversial Cave Paintings

Vocabulary Practice

A Write each word next to its correct definition. Then write its meaning in your language.

| prehistoric | hoax | authentic | hire |
| controversy | restore | document | accuse |

1. not copied; real or true   _____   _____

2. to give somebody a job   _____   _____

3. to blame someone for something wrong   _____   _____

4. a trick or lie that many people believe is true   _____   _____

5. to return someone or something to an earlier good condition   _____   _____

6. an issue that has many people for and against it   _____   _____

7. relating to the period before there were written records   _____   _____

8. to make a record of something through writing or photography   _____   _____

B Write the correct words to complete the sentences.

| dispute | fake | insult | pleasures |

1. Traveling is one of my greatest _____.

2. I never thought the bag was _____ until you said so.

3. She thinks paying him would be an _____ to their friendship.

4. They want to resolve the _____ between the management and the workers.

Writing Practice

A Unscramble the words to complete the sentences.

1. (honor / restored / Sautuola's / was)
   ▶ Fourteen years after he died, _____.

2. (to / them / read / excited / about / very)
   ▶ The public was _____.

3. (could / cavemen / not / made / such paintings / have)
   ▶ They said _____.

4. (hiring / of / a hoax / accused / to / a local artist / make)
   ▶ My father was even _____.

5. (were / believe / authentic / to / the paintings / refused)
   ▶ French archaeologists _____.

B Translate the sentences into your language, focusing on the meanings of the underlined parts.

1. I was the one <u>who</u> first noticed the shapes above us.
   ▶ _____

2. The scientific community <u>accepted</u> the Altamira cave paintings <u>as authentic</u>.
   ▶ _____

3. My father invited a professor from the University of Madrid <u>to help</u> him <u>document</u> the paintings.
   ▶ _____

Unit 18 37

Unit 19 Is Chocolate Good for You?

Vocabulary Practice

A Write each word next to its correct definition. Then write its meaning in your language.

bitter	run	conclusive	consume
contain	hype	cardiovascular	regularly

1. very often   _____ _____

2. not sweet   _____ _____

3. to eat or drink   _____ _____

4. to have or include something   _____ _____

5. to print or broadcast a news story   _____ _____

6. related to the heart and blood vessels   _____ _____

7. containing enough evidence to prove something   _____ _____

8. the use of a lot of advertisements to interest people   _____ _____

B Write the correct words to complete the sentences.

usually	decisive	eat	hype

1. What time do you _____ go to school?

2. There is a lot of _____ and marketing by big companies.

3. It is important for children to _____ breakfast before school.

4. More _____ actions will make a huge difference for our situation.

Writing Practice

A Unscramble the words to complete the sentences.

1. (to / likely / from / any / die / diseases)
   ▶ They were less _____.

2. (is / simply / that / hype / chocolate / healthy)
   ▶ Is the idea _____?

3. (that / chocolate / healthy / suggests / is / evidence)
   ▶ More and more _____.

4. (can / you / stay / eating chocolate / healthier / help)
   ▶ Many believe that _____.

5. (cacao / three / cups / to / four / drank / a day / of)
   ▶ The island natives _____.

B Translate the sentences into your language, focusing on the meanings of the underlined parts.

1. <u>Be sure to</u> check the labels carefully.
   ▶ _____

2. Some scientists say that <u>none of</u> these studies are really <u>conclusive</u>.
   ▶ _____

3. However, their relatives <u>who</u> left the island had <u>less healthy</u> cardiovascular systems.
   ▶ _____

Unit 20: What Was the Most Important Invention?

Vocabulary Practice

A Write each word or phrase next to its correct definition. Then write its meaning in your language.

carve	lecture	invention	clay
scholar	concept	generation	figure out

1. to understand or find an answer _____ _____

2. a general idea about something _____ _____

3. an expert in a field of knowledge _____ _____

4. all the people in a certain age group _____ _____

5. to talk to students to teach them a certain subject _____ _____

6. a heavy soil that becomes hard when it is dried _____ _____

7. to cut away at a hard surface to make a certain shape _____ _____

8. a machine or system that someone made for the first time _____ _____

B Write the correct words to complete the sentences.

talking	idea	invention	discovery

1. If you have an _____, just go for it and do it.

2. Scientists claim _____ of water on the planet.

3. The next speaker will be _____ about endangered birds.

4. As the saying goes, "Necessity is the mother of _____."

Writing Practice

A Unscramble the words to complete the sentences.

1. (down / they / write / know / what)
   ▶ Scholars _____.

2. (take / seem / a / may / time / long / to)
   ▶ Studying _____.

3. (no / reinvent / there / need / is / to / algebra)
   ▶ For example, _____.

4. (most / what / important / the / is / invention / on)
   ▶ Nobody really agrees _____.

5. (more / know / early / about / can / Chinese / the / we)
   ▶ Because of writing, _____.

B Translate the sentences into your language, focusing on the meanings of the underlined parts.

1. It is <u>faster than</u> trying to <u>figure things out</u> by yourself.
   ▶ _____

2. We can read about the ideas <u>that</u> great minds before us <u>took years to discover</u>.
   ▶ _____

3. <u>Once</u> humans started to write, they <u>could</u> give their knowledge to future generations.
   ▶ _____

Reading Voyage 2
BASIC

Reading Voyage is an eleven-level reading series divided into four stages: Starter, Basic, Plus, and Expert. The series is designed for high-beginner to low-advanced EFL students who want to enhance their reading abilities. The passages cover a wide range of topics that enable learners to expand their background knowledge. The various exercises will allow students to develop their reading comprehension, critical thinking, and vocabulary skills.

Key Features

- Appealing and informative texts covering a variety of topics
- Comprehension questions to help identify main ideas and details
- Reading Skill and Summary to help students analyze key concepts
- Vocabulary Expansion presenting synonyms, prefixes, and more
- Workbook for additional vocabulary and writing practice

Components

Student Book / Workbook

Download Resources at www.darakwon.co.kr :

MP3 files / Answer Key / Translations / Vocabulary lists

Scan this QR Code for MP3 files

Reading Voyage Series: BASIC

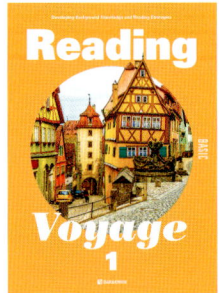
170-200 words

200-230 words

230-260 words